THE MANCHESTER UNIT FAMILY TREE

Written by Jim White

Devised and drawn by Pete Frame

With an Introduction by

Sir Bobby Charlton CBE

Manchester United Books

First published in 1996 by Manchester United Books
an imprint of André Deutsch Ltd, 106 Great Russell Street, London WC1B 3LJ
in association with
Manchester United Football Club Plc, Old Trafford, Manchester, M16 0RA

CIP data for this title is available from the British Library

ISBN 0 223 99025 9

Printed and bound in Great Britain by
Hillman Printers (Frome) Ltd, Frome, Somerset

Introduction

It would be impossible to estimate how many words have been printed about Manchester United over the years, such is their popularity across the globe. History books are particularly interesting, showing how United has grown from its humble beginnings to become the force it is today.

I have had the privilege of being associated with Manchester United for over forty years, virtually the same period that is covered by this fascinating book. It takes me back to my early days, signing professional forms on my seventeenth birthday, breaking into the first team in 1956 and scoring two goals on my debut against Charlton Athletic. It then moves through the years of recovery and revival after Munich to arguably the club's finest hour, the 1968 European Cup Final; I will treasure forever the memory of that magnificent night at Wembley Stadium.

The club has of course enjoyed many more moments of success, the majority coming in the last ten years under Alex Ferguson, a man who has worked so hard to restore the good and glorious traditions we became accustomed to under the late Sir Matt Busby.

The achievements of these two great Scots and the managers who served between them are well documented in Pete Frame's detailed charts. His family trees offer a new perspective on football history, piecing together the story of the modern Manchester United through the players who made it all happen.

The family tree is an appropriate device as United is to me an extended family anyway. With this book, the fan can read about the 'brothers' who together won the League Championships, the FA Cups and the European trophies. Football is of course a squad game, and the tree helps us to see this. Household names alone cannot win silverware so it's good to see the unsung heroes taking their rightful places in the book. From the Whitefoots, Viollets and Scanlons of the mid-1950s to the Irwins, Nevilles and Cantonas of the present day, all the players are here, side-by-side … united!

I hope you, the reader, glean as much pleasure from reading Pete Frame's work as I have.

SIR BOBBY CHARLTON CBE

Foreword

As a rock music journalist with an obsession for historical detail, I found it increasingly difficult to include all the relevant bumph without getting waist deep in convoluted prose – and this predicament spawned the idea of presenting information graphically, in the shape of family trees. This way I could trace the evolution of a particular group and include origins, personnel changes, ups and downs, record releases, chart appearances and anecdotes.

Early attempts were primitive. The first, a diagram of Blood Sweat & Tears drawn from *Zigzag* (the magazine I was editing at the time) in 1971, was little more than a crude framework hung with names and catalogue numbers – but after that, they got more and more complicated, as I strove to fill every square centimetre of paper.

I spent much of 1979–1982 cloistered up, doing little other than researching, interviewing, transcribing, plotting, drafting and toiling over the drawing board, putting together an anthology, *The Complete Rock Family Trees*, which eventually became a BBC2 television series in 1995.

After writing about rock music for 25 years, however, my brain began to feel like a cauliflower that had been left in the bottom of a cupboard for too long – and, for a change of scenery, I decided to write about my pre-rock 'n' roll passion, football. Having been born and raised in Luton, my first instinct was to do a Hatters family tree – but friends convinced me that this was not the best idea I'd ever had … so instead, with copious assistance from Old Trafford habitué Jim White, I did my second favourite team, Manchester United.

But watch out – I'm doing Luton next!

PETE FRAME

Acknowledgements

The author(s) would especially like to thank: Michael Crick (for being an unfailing oracle), Colin Hall (for designing the dummies), James Lovell (for asking the question in the car), James Pallister (for keeping his promises), Jim Phelan (for his love and efficiency) and John Whiston (for meeting us at The Dome and the use of his office).

THE
MANCHESTER UNITED
FAMILY TREE

By the start of the 1955-6 season, marvellous Manchester United had an unrivalled post-war record – and pundits firmly believed that nothing could stop them, so astute were Matt Busby and his roving talent scouts at finding precocious local lads, training and encouraging them, giving them a fair deal at all times, and welding the chosen few into a club of rare spirit as well as skill. Many joined straight from school; Colman, Edwards, Jones, Pegg, McGuinness, Doherty, Viollet and Scanlon all signed professional papers at 17; the whole team cost less than £50,000 to assemble! The sagacious Busby laid out money for only three players: £5000 for Wood, £15000 for Berry, and £29,999 for Taylor. (The odd quid was withheld so as not to lumber him with a burdensome 30 grand price tag!)

The greatest manager of the era, Matt Busby was born in Bellshill, Lanarkshire, on the 26th May 1909. Twenty years later, he moved to England, where he played for Manchester City and Liverpool, until the war saw him serving in the Army. During this period, he played for Scotland (at right half) fifteen times, eight of those as captain. In October 1945, he was appointed manager of United, and within three years led them to victory in the FA Cup. In 1952, they won the League championship for the first time since 1911! Of the 24 players who made appearances in the 1955-6 first team, 3 were from Ireland (Blanchflower, Whelan, Scott); I was from Wales (Webster); 3 from Yorkshire (Pegg, Jones, Taylor); I from Darlington (Wood); I from Dudley (Edwards); I Brummie (Berry). The other 14 had all grown up in Lancashire.

1955-56

Champions! United ended the season top of the league...so far ahead that rivals needed binoculars to see them! They were eleven points clear – the biggest margin for almost 60 years.

Since last topping Division One – only 4 years earlier – Matt Busby had revamped the team so comprehensively that only Byrne and Berry remained. Byrne had succeeded Chilton as the team captain.

JEFF WHITEFOOT	EDDIE LEWIS	JACK CROMPTON	WALTER WHITEHURST	JACKIE SCOTT	BILL FOULKES	DENNIS VIOLLET	ALBERT SCANLON	WILF McGUINNESS
right half 15 games	centre forward 4 games 1 goal	goalkeeper 1 game	right half 1 game	outside right 1 game	right back 26 games	inside left 34 games 20 goals	outside left 6 games 1 goal	left half 3 games 1 goal
to Grimsby Town 11/57	to Preston in 12/55 for £10,000	to Luton Town 10/56 as trainer	to Chesterfield in 11/56	to Grimsby Town 6/56				

The five new players who made their first team debut during the 1956-7 season had all played for England Schoolboys. For the two goalies, replacing Ray Wood was a hopeless quest and neither found a chance to shine. Clayton, from Staffordshire, spent 6 years at United – but managed only two appearances. A Yorkshire lad, Hawksworth was away doing his National Service when called back for his only game – at Blackpool. Ronnie Cope joined from Crewe Schoolboys; he'd been on United's professional staff for five years when he got to make his debut, against Arsenal. For Alex Dawson, dreams came true: he crossed the country from Humberside to sign with United a few days after his 17th birthday...and on his debut only weeks later, scored in front of the home crowd. He then scored in each of the season's two remaining matches...a league champion!

Busby's fifth debutant was one of his greatest discoveries, the bold marauder...Bobby Charlton. The son of a Northumberland coal miner, he joined United as an amateur in Jan 53, going pro on his 17th birthday, on 11-10-54. He wore the first team shirt for the first time in Oct 56 and began to show his prowess immediately, banging in two goals ...against Charlton Athletic. On that occasion he played at centre forward, in place of the indisposed Tommy Taylor – but when Taylor returned to the side the following week, Charlton switched to inside left, vying with Dennis Viollet to hold the position. In his first season, Charlton scored 10 goals – in only 14 games. Viollet racked up 16, and Taylor 22 ...but the leading scorer was Liam Whelan. He managed 26 league goals, plus 4 during the FA Cup run, and 3 more in the European Cup.

1956-57

Busby's finest season! League champions for the second year running, eight points ahead of nearest rivals Spurs. His junior team won the FA Youth Cup for the fifth year in succession. What a time it was!

At the beginning of Feb 57, a crowd of almost 64000 watched the local City/United derby. City were on a roll: two years earlier centre forward Don Revie had introduced his revolutionary 'Revie Plan', which helped them to

TONY HAWKSWORTH	GORDON CLAYTON	RONNIE COPE	ALEX DAWSON	BOBBY CHARLTON	BILL FOULKES	DENNIS VIOLLET	ALBERT SCANLON	WILF McGUINNESS
goalkeeper 1 game	goalkeeper 2 games	centre half 2 games	centre forward 3 games 3 goals	inside left 14 games 10 goals	right back 39 games	inside left 27 games 16 goals	outside left 5 games 2 goals	left half 13 games
quit pro football 12/58	to Tranmere Rovers 11/59 for £2000							

1955–56

Back Row (l/r)
Duncan Edwards, Bill Foulkes, Mark Jones, Ray Wood, Eddie Colman, David Pegg

Front Row (l/r)
Johnny Berry, Liam Whelan, Roger Byrne, Tommy Taylor, Dennis Viollet

With an average age of just 22, they became affectionately known as "the Busby Babes." The reserve team also topped the Central League - by 5 points - and the even younger Babes took the

FA Youth Cup, which they had held since the competition started in 1953. The first team's championship assault was propelled by a superabundance of goals from twin strikers Viollet and Taylor.

The season's only black spot was their ignominious departure from the FA Cup, in the third round, which they lost to Bristol Rovers, 0-4. Those of us who saw The Busby Babes felt that we would

never see their like again. When they came to Luton in Feb 56, it was like a visit by Bill Haley, Marlon Brando, Marilyn Monroe, Roy Rogers, Winston Churchill, the Queen, Lonnie Donegan and Davy Crockett - all at

once! The only bummer for me was the non-appearance of Duncan Edwards, the coolest player of his generation. Weird thing: only 16000 attended the game.

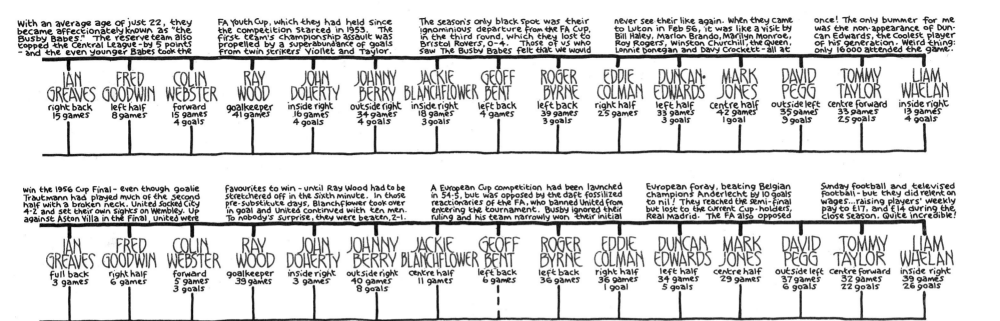

IAN GREAVES	FRED GOODWIN	COLIN WEBSTER	RAY WOOD	JOHN DOHERTY	JOHNNY BERRY	JACKIE BLANCHFLOWER	GEOFF BENT	ROGER BYRNE	EDDIE COLMAN	DUNCAN EDWARDS	MARK JONES	DAVID PEGG	TOMMY TAYLOR	LIAM WHELAN
right back	left half	forward	goalkeeper	inside right	outside right	inside right	left back	left back	right half	left half	centre half	outside left	centre forward	inside right
15 games	8 games	15 games 4 goals	41 games	16 games 4 goals	34 games 4 goals	18 games 3 goals	4 games	39 games 3 goals	25 games	33 games 3 goals	42 games 1 goal	35 games 9 goals	33 games 25 goals	13 games 4 goals

win the 1956 Cup Final - even though goalie Trautmann had played much of the second half with a broken neck. United socked City 4-2 and set their own sights on Wembley. Up against Aston Villa in the Final, United were

favourites to win - until Ray Wood had to be stretchered off in the sixth minute. In those pre-substitute days, Blanchflower took over in goal and United continued with ten men. To nobody's surprise, they were beaten, 2-1.

A European Cup competition had been launched in 54-5, but was opposed by the daft fossilized reactionaries of the FA, who banned United from entering the tournament. Busby ignored their ruling and his team narrowly won their initial

European foray, beating Belgian champions Anderlecht by 10 goals to nil! They reached the semi-final but lost to the current Cup-holders, Real Madrid. The FA also opposed

Sunday football and televised football - but they did relent on wages...raising players' weekly pay to £17, and £14 during the close season. Quite incredible!

IAN GREAVES	FRED GOODWIN	COLIN WEBSTER	RAY WOOD	JOHN DOHERTY	JOHNNY BERRY	JACKIE BLANCHFLOWER	GEOFF BENT	ROGER BYRNE	EDDIE COLMAN	DUNCAN EDWARDS	MARK JONES	DAVID PEGG	TOMMY TAYLOR	LIAM WHELAN
full back	right half	forward	goalkeeper	inside right	outside right	centre half	left back	left back	right half	left half	centre half	outside left	centre forward	inside right
3 games	6 games	5 games 3 goals	39 games	3 games	40 games 8 goals	11 games	6 games	36 games	36 games 1 goal	34 games 5 goals	29 games	37 games 6 goals	32 games 22 goals	39 games 26 goals

1956–57

Back Row (l/r)
Bill Ingles, Geoff Bent, Ray Wood, Mark Jones, Bill Foulkes, Dennis Viollet, Tom Curry

Middle Row (l/r)
Jackie Blanchflower, Colin Webster, Wilf McGuinness, Tommy Taylor, Liam Whelan, David Pegg

Foreground
Johnny Berry

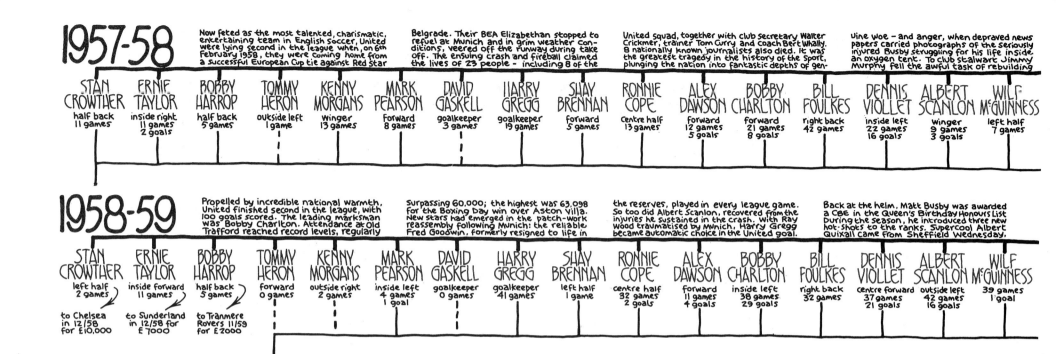

1957-58

Now feted as the most talented, charismatic, entertaining team in English soccer, United were lying second in the league when, on 6th February 1958, they were coming home from a successful European Cup tie against Red Star

Belgrade. Their BEA Elizabethan stopped to refuel at Munich and in grim weather conditions, veered off the runway during take off. The ensuing crash and fireball claimed the lives of 23 people - including 8 of the

United squad, together with club secretary Walter Crickmer, trainer Tom Curry and coach Bert Whally. 8 nationally known journalists also died. It was the greatest tragedy in the history of the sport, plunging the nation into fantastic depths of gen-

uine woe - and anger, when depraved news papers carried photographs of the seriously injured Busby struggling for his life inside an oxygen tent. To club stalwart Jimmy Murphy fell the awful task of rebuilding

STAN CROWTHER	ERNIE TAYLOR	BOBBY HARROP	TOMMY HERON	KENNY MORGANS	MARK PEARSON	DAVID GASKELL	HARRY GREGG	SHAY BRENNAN	RONNIE COPE	ALEX DAWSON	BOBBY CHARLTON	BILL FOULKES	DENNIS VIOLLET	ALBERT SCANLON	WILF McGUINNESS
half back 11 games	inside right 11 games 2 goals	half back 5 games	outside left 1 game	Winger 13 games	Forward 8 games	goalkeeper 3 games	goalkeeper 19 games	forward 5 games	Centre half 13 games	forward 12 games 5 goals	forward 21 games 8 goals	right back 42 games	inside left 22 games 16 goals	winger 9 games 3 goals	left half 7 games

1958-59

Propelled by incredible national warmth, United finished second in the league, with 100 goals scored. The leading marksman was Bobby Charlton. Attendance at Old Trafford reached record levels, regularly

Surpassing 60,000; the highest was 63,098 for the Boxing Day win over Aston Villa. New stars had emerged in the patch-work reassembly following Munich: the reliable Fred Goodwin, formerly resigned to life in

the reserves, played in every league game. So too did Albert Scanlon, recovered from the injuries he sustained in the crash. With Ray Wood traumatised by Munich, Harry Gregg became automatic choice in the United goal.

Back at the helm, Matt Busby was awarded a CBE in the Queen's Birthday Honours List During the season, he introduced three new hot-shots to the ranks. Supercool Albert Quixall came from Sheffield Wednesday,

STAN CROWTHER	ERNIE TAYLOR	BOBBY HARROP	TOMMY HERON	KENNY MORGANS	MARK PEARSON	DAVID GASKELL	HARRY GREGG	SHAY BRENNAN	RONNIE COPE	ALEX DAWSON	BOBBY CHARLTON	BILL FOULKES	DENNIS VIOLLET	ALBERT SCANLON	WILF McGUINNESS
left half 2 games	inside forward 11 games	half back 5 games	forward 0 games	outside right 2 games	inside left 4 games 1 goal	goalkeeper 0 games	goalkeeper 41 games	left half 1 game	centre half 32 games	forward 11 games 4 goals	inside left 38 games 29 goals	right back 32 games	centre forward 37 games 21 goals	outside left 42 games 16 goals	39 games 1 goal
to Chelsea in 12/58 for £10,000	to Sunderland in 12/58 for £7000	to Tranmere Rovers 11/59 for £2000													

1957–58

Back Row (l/r)
Fred Goodwin, Alex Dawson, Ronnie Cope, Harry Gregg, Ian Greaves, Stan Crowther

Front Row (l/r)
Dennis Viollet, Ernie Taylor, Bill Foulkes, Colin Webster, Bobby Charlton, Mark Pearson

the team. It is a measure of the club spirit and the enthusiasm of their supporters that despite the disaster, United met every one of their commitments and only two games had to be postponed. A stopgap team fought on with improbable abandon, thrilling hearts by reaching the FA Cup Final - but a fairytale ending to a grim story was denied them when Bolton Wanderers triumphed 2-0. Wolves, led by the redoubtable Billy Wright, swiped their First Division championship crown, while the Wolves youth team beat the United lads and went on to take the FA Youth Cup away from the United trophy room for the first time since 1953. Real Madrid won the European Cup for the third year in succession; United reached the semi-final but were bumped out by Milan. The Munich disaster also affected the England team, who were unable to recapture the panache they'd had with Byrne, Edwards and Taylor in the side.

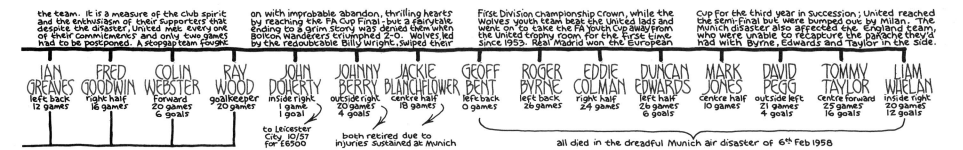

IAN GREAVES	FRED GOODWIN	COLIN WEBSTER	RAY WOOD	JOHN DOHERTY	JOHNNY BERRY	JACKIE BLANCHFLOWER	GEOFF BENT	ROGER BYRNE	EDDIE COLMAN	DUNCAN EDWARDS	MARK JONES	DAVID PEGG	TOMMY TAYLOR	LIAM WHELAN
left back 12 games	right half 16 games	forward 20 games 6 goals	goalkeeper 20 games	inside right 1 game 1 goal	outside right 20 games 4 goals	centre half 18 games	left back 0 games	left back 26 games	right half 24 games	left half 26 games 6 goals	centre half 10 games	outside left 21 games 4 goals	centre forward 25 games 16 goals	inside right 20 games 12 goals

to Leicester City 10/57 for £6500

both retired due to injuries sustained at Munich

all died in the dreadful Munich air disaster of 6th Feb 1958

where he had an Elvis Presley hairstyle before Elvis did. Busby laid out £45000 for him - a UK transfer fee record - but he had some trouble getting started, scoring only 4 goals in his first season. Joe Carolan, who had been on the books since Feb 56, when he left Dublin, graduated to the top team a couple of months after his 21st birthday, and Warren Bradley joined from the amateur club Bishop Auckland, to whack in 12 goals. The surprise of the season, he was also selected to play for England - who, the tabloids opined, were rubbish!

During the 1957-8 season, ten players made their United debut - four before the Munich crash. Kenny Morgans, David Gaskell and Peter Jones were fledgling "babes" who'd gone pro with United after leaving school - in April 56, Oct 57 and April 55 respectively. Harry Gregg joined from Doncaster Rovers in Dec 57 - for a transfer fee of £25,000 - a world record for a goalkeeper. After Munich, acting manager Jimmy Murphy acquired only 3 new players to bolster up the team: 32 year old Ernie Taylor joined from Blackpool at a cost of £8000; 22 year old Stan Crowther joined from Aston Villa and was playing for United before the ink on his contract had dried; Tommy Heron, also 22, signed from the Irish club Portadown. Also raised to first team status were 3 more youngsters who'd been playing for the youth and reserve teams: Bobby Harrop, Shay Brennan and Mark Pearson, who had been on United's professional books since May 54, April 55, and May 57 respectively. In the first post-Munich game, a cuptie against Sheffield Wednesday, Brennan scored twice on his debut. Alex Dawson also got a story book result in the semi-final replay against Fulham when he banged in three goals - the youngest (at 18 years and 33 days) player to score a hat trick since pre World War II!

For the second year running, the FA saw fit to raise players' wages. Those over the age of 20 now got £20 a week during the playing season and £17 a week in the close season. This was not enough for the Welsh international star John Charles, who joined Juventus for a fee of £65000 - of which he got ten grand!

IAN GREAVES	FRED GOODWIN	ALBERT QUIXALL	WARREN BRADLEY	JOE CAROLAN	COLIN WEBSTER	RAY WOOD	REG HUNTER
full back 34 games	right half 42 games 6 goals	inside right 33 games 4 goals	outside right 24 games 12 goals	left back 23 games	forward 7 games 5 goals	goalkeeper 1 game	outside right 1 game

to Swansea Town 10/58 for £7500

to Huddersfield Town 12/58 for £1500

to Wrexham 2/60

1958–59

Back Row (l/r)
Bill Foulkes, Jackie Blanchflower, Fred Goodwin, Eddie Lewis, Albert Scanlon, Ronnie Cope

Front Row (l/r)
Johnny Berry, Colin Webster, Jack Crompton, Wilf McGuinness, Bobby Charlton

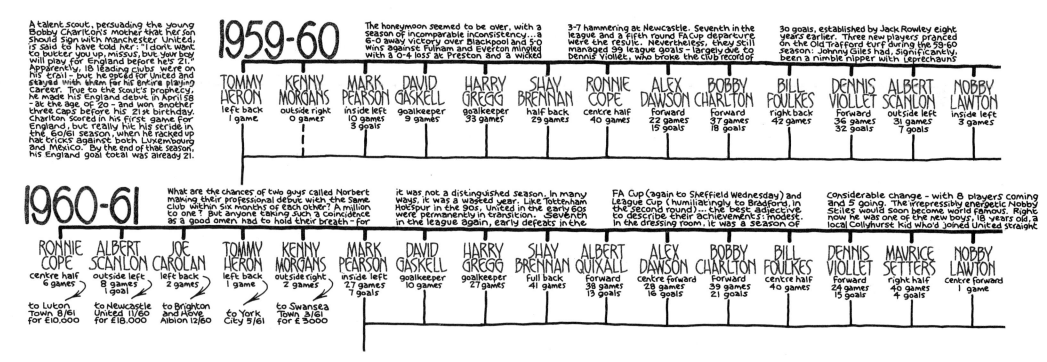

1959-60

A talent scout, persuading the young Bobby Charlton's mother that her son should sign with Manchester United, is said to have told her: "I don't want to butter you up, missus, but your boy will play for England before he's 21." Apparently, 18 leading clubs were on his trail – but he opted for United and stayed with them for his entire playing career. True to the scout's prophecy, he made his England debut in April 58 – at the age of 20 – and won another three caps before his 21st birthday. Charlton scored in his first game for England, but really hit his stride in the 60/61 season, when he racked up hat tricks against both Luxembourg and Mexico. By the end of that season, his England goal total was already 21.

The honeymoon seemed to be over, with a season of incomparable inconsistency...a 6-0 away victory over Blackpool and 5-0 wins against Fulham and Everton mingled with a 0-4 loss at Preston and a wicked 3-7 hammering at Newcastle. Seventh in the league and a fifth round FA Cup departure were the result. Nevertheless, they still managed 99 league goals – largely due to Dennis Viollet, who broke the club record of 30 goals, established by Jack Rowley eight years earlier. Three new players pranced on the Old Trafford turf during the 59-60 season: Johnny Giles had, significantly, been a nimble nipper with Leprechauns

TOMMY HERON	KENNY MORGANS	MARK PEARSON	DAVID GASKELL	HARRY GREGG	SHAY BRENNAN	RONNIE COPE	ALEX DAWSON	BOBBY CHARLTON	BILL FOULKES	DENNIS VIOLLET	ALBERT SCANLON	NOBBY LAWTON
left back 1 game	outside right 0 games	inside left 10 games 3 goals	goalkeeper 9 games	goalkeeper 33 games	half back 29 games	centre half 40 games	forward 22 games 15 goals	forward 37 games 18 goals	right back 42 games	forward 36 games 32 goals	outside left 31 games 7 goals	inside left 3 games

1960-61

What are the chances of two guys called Norbert making their professional debut with the same club within six months of each other? A million to one? But anyone taking such a coincidence as a good omen had to hold their breath – for it was not a distinguished season. In many ways, it was a wasted year. Like Tottenham Hotspur in the 90s, United in the early 60s were permanently in transition. Seventh in the league again, early defeats in the FA Cup (again to Sheffield Wednesday) and League Cup (humiliatingly to Bradford, in the second round)...the best adjective to describe their achievements: modest. In the dressing room, it was a season of considerable change – with 8 players coming and 5 going. The irrepressibly energetic Nobby Stiles would soon become world famous. Right now he was one of the new boys, 18 years old, a local Collyhurst kid who'd joined United straight

RONNIE COPE	ALBERT SCANLON	JOE CAROLAN	TOMMY HERON	KENNY MORGANS	MARK PEARSON	DAVID GASKELL	HARRY GREGG	SHAY BRENNAN	ALBERT QUIXALL	ALEX DAWSON	BOBBY CHARLTON	BILL FOULKES	DENNIS VIOLLET	MAURICE SETTERS	NOBBY LAWTON
centre half 6 games	outside left 8 games 1 goal	left back 2 games	left back 1 game	outside right 2 games	inside left 27 games 7 goals	goalkeeper 10 games	goalkeeper 27 games	full back 41 games	forward 38 games 13 goals	centre forward 28 games 16 goals	forward 39 games 21 goals	centre half 40 games	forward 24 games 15 goals	right half 40 games 4 goals	centre forward 1 game
to Luton Town 8/61 for £10,000	to Newcastle United 11/60 for £18,000	to Brighton and Hove Albion 12/60	to York City 5/61	to Swansea Town 3/61 for £3000											

1959–60

Back Row (l/r)
Bobby English, Shay Brennan, Gordon Clayton, Alex Dawson, Tony Hawksworth, Fred Goodwin, Ray Wood, Bobby Harrop, Joe Carolan

Middle Row (l/r)
Ted Dalton, Jimmy Murphy, Barry Smith, Harry Gregg, Jimmy Elms, Harold Bratt, Reg Holland, Mark Pearson, Stan Crowther, Ronnie Cope, Ian Greaves, Warren Bradley, Tommy Heron, Wilf McGuinness, Jimmy Shiels, Johnny Giles, Bill Inglis, Jack Crompton

Front Row (l/r)
Ernie Taylor, Colin Webster, Bill Foulkes, Matt Busby, Kenny Morgans, Albert Scanlon, Dennis Viollet, Bobby Charlton

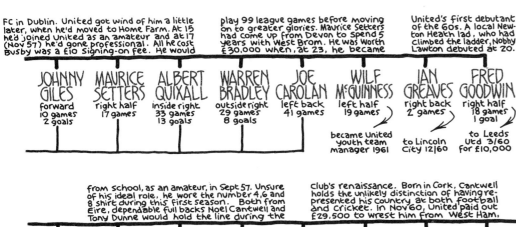

FC in Dublin. United got wind of him a little later, when he'd moved to Home Farm. At 15 he'd joined United as an amateur and at 17 (Nov 57) he'd gone professional. All he cost Busby was a £10 signing-on fee. He would play 99 league games before moving on to greater glories. Maurice Setters had come up from Devon to spend 5 years with West Brom. He was worth £30,000 when, at 23, he became United's first debutant of the 60s. A local Newton Heath lad, who had climbed the ladder, Nobby Lawton debuted at 20.

Three stalwarts, who between them racked up over 260 league and cup appearances, played their last games for United: Fred Goodwin, Ian Greaves and Wilf McGuinness - the prodigiously talented schoolboy who joined United the same day as Bobby Charlton. His playing career was tragically halted by a compound leg fracture in December 59. He would take over the management of the United youth team ...and, ten years later, of the first team.

It was during the 59/60 season that more supporters were able to avoid the notorious Manchester rain: the Stretford End was covered in - giving shelter to some 22000 on the terraces. By this time, Old Trafford also benefited from recent flood-lights.

At the end of the decade, Wilf McGuinness would succeed Matt Busby as manager of the most illustrious footballing side in Britain. It was a position few men had held. Ernest Mangnall created the first legendary team, presiding from 1903 to 1912. When he defected to Manchester City, he was replaced by John Robson, who stayed through the war until, in 1921, ill-health forced him to step aside in favour of John Chapman. Accused of hanky panky (FA allegations which they never revealed), Chapman walked in 1926 and for 6 months Clarrie Hilditch filled the breach as United's one and only player manager. In quick succession came Herbert Bamlett, Walter Crickmer, Scott Duncan... and World War II. When normal service was resumed, the man in charge was Matt Busby.

JOHNNY GILES — forward — 10 games — 2 goals

MAURICE SETTERS — right half — 17 games

ALBERT QUIXALL — inside right — 33 games — 13 goals

WARREN BRADLEY — outside right — 29 games — 8 goals

JOE CAROLAN — left back — 41 games

WILF McGUINNESS — left half — 19 games → became United youth team manager 1961

IAN GREAVES — right back — 2 games → to Lincoln City 12/60

FRED GOODWIN — right half — 18 games — 1 goal → to Leeds Utd 3/60 for £10,000

from school, as an amateur, in Sept 57. Unsure of his ideal role, he wore the number 4, 6 and 8 shirt during this first season. Both from Eire, dependable full backs Noel Cantwell and Tony Dunne would hold the line during the club's renaissance. Born in Cork, Cantwell holds the unlikely distinction of having represented his country at both football and cricket. In Nov 60, United paid out £29,500 to wrest him from West Ham, where he'd spent the previous eight years. Considering he was to play well over 500 games for United, Dunne was one of Matt Busby's great bargain basement selections, costing only £5000 when he left the Dublin club Shelbourne in April 60. Frank Haydock from Eccles, Ian Moir from Aberdeen and Jimmy Nicholson from Belfast had all started with United as amateurs - and all got their first team chance during the early part of the season.

JOHNNY GILES — forward — 23 games — 2 goals

NOBBY STILES — rover — 26 games — 2 goals

NOEL CANTWELL — left back — 24 games

WARREN BRADLEY — outside right — 4 games

TONY DUNNE — full back — 3 games

IAN MOIR — winger — 8 games — 1 goal

JIMMY NICHOLSON — left half — 31 games — 5 goals

FRANK HAYDOCK — centre half — 4 games

RONNIE BRIGGS — goalkeeper — 1 game

MIKE PINNER — goalkeeper — 4 games → ultimately went pro with Leyton Orient

What would novice goalkeeper Ronnie Briggs give to erase Jan 61 from his life? A former Irish Schoolboy international, he signed professional papers with United on his 17th birthday. 9 months later, with both Gregg and Gaskell indisposed, he underwent the most terrifying baptism by fire...conceding 6 goals on his debut, away at Leicester, and another 7 in his next game (in front of the Old Trafford crowd), that notorious cup fixture against Sheffield Wednesday. The hapless chap was promptly pulled and rested! Mike Pinner was summoned as an emergency measure. An experienced amateur who had played for England many times, he held the fort for 4 games, admitting only 5 goals. Happily, David Gaskell recovered sufficiently to play the remaining games.

1960–61

Back Row (l/r)
Maurice Setters, Bill Foulkes, Ronnie Cope, Harry Gregg, Albert Scanlon, Bobby Charlton

Front Row (l/r)
Warren Bradley, Albert Quixall, Dennis Viollet, Shay Brennan, Joe Carolan

The whole face of English soccer changed in 1962, when the FA finally agreed to abolish the maximum wage. They had been severely rattled by the defection of several top players - most notably Jimmy Greaves of Chelsea and Denis Law of Manchester City, who signed with the Italian clubs AC Milan and Torino for unimaginable transfer fees, salaries and perks. Once the lid was off, it was only a matter of time before widespread mayhem started breaking out in the football league. Everyone wanted a slice, and as clubs began to pay higher wages to their star players, the lower paid complained. It would all work out OK, but many clubs cut down on their pro staff, setting a pattern for the future, when the emphasis would be on quality rather than quantity. Until then, it had been fame, glory, achievement, passion, love, pride, patriotism, ambition, the thrill of running out of the tunnel to the cheers of thousands of doughty fans. It was never money. Most players lived in council houses. They were erstwhile coalmen and fitters who knew they would never make any more than twenty quid a week playing football. But now they could. Previously a precarious living, soccer had career potential!

1961-62

Oh dear. The mix was not working. Crowds at Old Trafford touched post-war depths. Only 20,807 could be bothered to turn up for the game against Aston Villa in January. The glory that was the Busby Babes was long forgotten as the team completed an autumnal run of ten league matches without a win. In the dressing room there was dissent, on the pitch failure, and on the terraces gloom. It was the same wherever you went: profound

PHIL CHISNALL	DAVID GASKELL	HARRY GREGG	SHAY BRENNAN	ALBERT QUIXALL	TONY DUNNE	BOBBY CHARLTON	BILL FOULKES	DAVID HERD	MAURICE SETTERS
outside right 9 games 1 goal	goalkeeper 21 games	goalkeeper 13 games	right back 41 games 2 goals	forward 21 games 10 goals	left back 28 games	outside left 37 games 8 goals	centre half 40 games	forward 27 games 14 goals	half back 38 games 3 goals

United were the first team to benefit from the FA's wage derestriction: Matt Busby was able to make Denis Law an offer he couldn't refuse. Born in Aberdeen, the fitba' crazy Law had gone professional with Huddersfield Town (of all people!), signing on his 17th birthday in February 57. 18 months later, he was playing for Scotland - their youngest post-war cap - scoring on his debut against Wales. In March 60, Manchester City secured him for £53,000 but his street value had almost doubled by June 61, when Torino convinced him that his future lay in Italy. They paid £100,000 - but he only stayed a year. In August 62, Busby shelled out the record fee of £110,000 to get him into a United shirt... "and he was worth every penny!"

1962-63

Seven minutes into his first game for United, Denis Law scored. It seemed to be a pledge... Law became the hero, the star, the talisman that would turn the club around, the key to their transformation. This season, Busby spent more money on new players than he had in the previous three put together - and he only bought two! Pat Crerand, a Glaswegian, was the other. Another Scottish international, he joined from Celtic in Feb 63, after a cheque for £56,000 had changed hands. The only other player to make his debut was Denis Walker, former captain of the Cheshire Schoolboys team, who made his one and only appearance in the last game of the

DENIS LAW	PAT CRERAND	PHIL CHISNALL	DAVID GASKELL	HARRY GREGG	SHAY BRENNAN	ALBERT QUIXALL	TONY DUNNE	BOBBY CHARLTON	BILL FOULKES	DAVID HERD	MAURICE SETTERS
forward 38 games 23 goals	right half 19 games	forward 6 games 1 goal	goalkeeper 18 games	goalkeeper 24 games	right back 37 games	forward 31 games 7 goals	full back 25 games	outside left 28 games 7 goals	centre half 41 games	centre forward 37 games 19 goals	left half 27 games 1 goal

1961–62

Back Row (l/r)
Noel Cantwell, Bobby Charlton, David Gaskell, Bill Foulkes, Albert Quixall

Middle Row (l/r)
Matt Busby, Jimmy Nicholson, Shay Brennan, Phil Chisnall, Jack Crompton

Front Row (l/r)
Johnny Giles, David Herd, Maurice Setters, Tony Dunne

Foreground (l/r)
Nobby Stiles, Nobby Lawton

widespread sadness (because United's fanbase stretched from Cornwall to the Highlands) that the most illustrious football team in Britain had lost the plot. The only bright spell in a season in which they finished 15th in the league was

a decent Cup run – ended in the semi-final by Spurs. Though new inspiration was now clearly needed, only 3 players debuted during the 61-2 season. A Stretford lad, Phil Chisnall had been on the books since

he left school in 1958, playing in the youth team and the reserves – and the Belfast born Sammy McMillan followed the same route, making a pretty impressive leap to senior football

by bagging six goals in his first season. The only player moving Busby to dip into his purse was David Herd – acquired from Arsenal in July 61 for £35000. Born just a stone's throw from Busby in Lanark-

shire, but raised in Moss Side, Herd was 17 when he made his debut for Stockport County – alongside his 39 year old father. He joined Arsenal in Aug 54; returned north 7 years later.

NOBBY STILES	NOEL CANTWELL	IAN MOIR	NOBBY LAWTON	JOHNNY GILES	MARK PEARSON	FRANK HAYDOCK	JIMMY NICHOLSON	SAMMY McMILLAN	RONNIE BRIGGS	DENNIS VIOLLET	ALEX DAWSON	WARREN BRADLEY
rover 34 games 7 goals	left back 17 games 2 goals	winger 9 games	forward 20 games 6 goals	forward 30 games 6 goals	forward 17 games 2 goals	centre half 1 game	half back 17 games	forward 11 games 6 goals	goalkeeper 8 games → to Swansea Town 5/64	forward 13 games 7 goals → to Stoke City 1/62 for £25,000	centre forward 4 games 2 goals → to Preston in 10/61 for £18,000	outside right 6 games → to Bury in 3/62 for £40,000

Briggs, Viollet, Dawson and Bradley all played their last games for United during the 61/62 season. Dennis Viollet's sudden departure, after 11 years plus as a pro, mystified the pundits almost as much as the fact that he had only been selected to play for England twice, despite his 178 goals for the club. One of the few players of his day with any academic qualifications, Warren Bradley became a headmaster on hanging up his boots.

season. The first black to play for United, he was also one of seven players who moved on...including Johnny Giles, who went on to score 115 goals for Leeds. "A bad mistake, letting him go." said Busby.

The winter of 62-3 was one of the worst in living memory. Many games had to be postponed as snow and ice hung around for ever. Law must have wished he was back in Italy - especially when United

lurched from one disastrous game to another, losing 20...and only managing to escape relegation by 3 points. They ended up 19th in the league – but won the Cup Final!

Their victory in the 1963 Cup Final was the biggest boost to United morale since they'd topped the First Division in successive years, back in 1956 and 57. The odds had been in favour of their opponents, Leicester City, who'd finished 4th in the league and now seemed invincible with goalkeeper Gordon Banks in top form... but Munich survivors Foulkes and Charlton, who'd had to make do with losers' medals in the 1957 and 58 finals, were not about to leave the field with their tails dragging a third time. It was Law who opened the scoring, then Herd slammed in two more to ensure that it was Noel Cantwell who held the Cup high for the cheering 100,000 at Wembley.

At the start of the decade, the press lambasted the England team selectors for their lack of consistency, vision, strategy and competence - but this was all forgotten a few months later when everything suddenly jelled in a flurry of victories. During the 60/61 season, England played remarkably, not only beating Spain 4-2, Mexico 8-0, and Luxembourg 9-0, but also winning all the home internationals, scoring 19 goals in 3 matches, including 9 against Scotland. The only home team to qualify for the 1962 World Cup, England were knocked out in the quarter final - by Brazil, who went on to beat Czechoslovakia in the final. Never mind, only 4 years to wait until we get another crack.

NOBBY STILES	NOEL CANTWELL	IAN MOIR	NOBBY LAWTON	JOHNNY GILES	MARK PEARSON	FRANK HAYDOCK	JIMMY NICHOLSON	SAMMY McMILLAN	DENNIS WALKER
rover 31 games 2 goals	left back 25 games 1 goal	winger 9 games 1 goal	rover 12 games → to Preston N.E. 3/63	forward 36 games 4 goals → to Leeds Utd 8/63 for £37,500	forward 2 games → to Sheffield Wed 10/63 for £20,000	centre half 1 game → to Charlton Ath 8/63 for £10,000	half back 10 games → to Huddersfield Town 12/64 for £8000	outside left 4 games → to Wrexham 12/63 for £8000	outside left 1 game → to York City 4/64

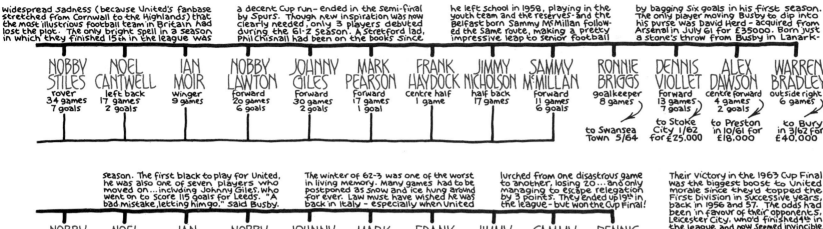

1962–63

Back Row (l/r)
Maurice Setters, Jimmy Nicholson, David Gaskell, Shay Brennan, Mark Pearson, Noel Cantwell

Middle Row (l/r)
Bill Foulkes, Sammy McMillan, Tony Dunne, Nobby Stiles, Nobby Lawton

Front Row (l/r)
Johnny Giles, Albert Quixall, David Herd, Denis Law, Bobby Charlton

During the early 60s, United's principal bête noire was Tottenham Hotspur. In the 60/61 season, Spurs made 20th century history by winning the double - Football League Champions and FA Cup Winners. The last club to manage this feat had been Aston Villa, back in 1897... so Spurs were cock-a-hoop. A year later, they lost the league title to little old Ipswich Town (who had only been promoted from the Second Division the previous season, after escaping Division Three in 1957), but they won the FA Cup for the second year running. In 62/63, Spurs ruled the roost when they beat Athletico Madrid, 5-1, to win the European Cup Winners Cup... but their luck ran out in the same competition the following year, when they were knocked out by United. Any celebrations were premature, however. A burst of 3 goals in 7 minutes put paid to their hopes. Having won the first leg of the quarter final against Sporting Club of Lisbon 4-1, United lost the second leg 5-0!

1963-64

Their renaissance finally underway, United finished the 63/64 season First Division runners up - behind Liverpool, currently cresting on the Merseybeat wave - but hopes of retaining the Cup were dashed when they lost the semi-final to West Ham. Netting 30 goals in as many league matches, Law was leading scorer again - notching up 10 more in the cup run and another 6 in Europe. No-one disputed his selection as The European Player of the Year. Matt Busby continued the policy of buying in talent from other First Division clubs while simultaneously developing local youngsters. Two players made their first and last appearance

ALBERT QUIXALL	PHIL CHISNALL	DAVID GASKELL	HARRY GREGG	SHAY BRENNAN	DENIS LAW	TONY DUNNE	BOBBY CHARLTON	BILL FOULKES	DAVID HERD	MAURICE SETTERS	NOBBY STILES
forward 9 games 3 goals	forward 20 games 6 goals	goalkeeper 17 games	goalkeeper 25 games	right back 17 games	inside left 30 games 30 goals	full back 40 games	forward 40 games 9 goals	centre half 41 games 1 goal	forward 30 games 20 goals	left half 32 games 4 goals	rover 17 games
to Oldham Athletic 9/64 for £8500	to Liverpool in 4/64 for £25,000										

1964-65

Champions! Going one better than last season, United won their first League title in 8 years, beating runners-up Leeds, deliciously, by goal average. The championship was stimulated by an autumnal sequence of 13 wins and a draw. These coincided with the arrival of Pat Dunne, a £10,500 acquisition from Shamrock Rovers. He wasn't an earth-shaking goalkeeper but his Shamrock had four leaves. One of 4 debutants, he was joined in the first team squad by three Johns: Aston, Fitzpatrick and Connelly. Aston's father had played a stoical role in United's post-war triumphs and after a ten year gap, John Jr followed along, starting as a school leaver working on the ground staff. The Aberdonian Fitzpatrick too had progressed from the ground staff, costing no more than a signing-on fee - while Connelly was the season's extravagant investment, costing £60,000 when he moved

PAT DUNNE	JOHN CONNELLY	JOHN FITZPATRICK	JOHN ASTON	NOEL CANTWELL	WILLIE ANDERSON	DAVID GASKELL	HARRY GREGG	SHAY BRENNAN	DENIS LAW	TONY DUNNE	BOBBY CHARLTON	BILL FOULKES	DAVID HERD	GEORGE BEST	DAVID SADLER
goalkeeper 37 games	outside right 42 games 15 goals	half back 2 games	outside left 1 game	centre forward 2 games 1 goal	outside right 0 games	goalkeeper 5 games	goalkeeper 0 games	right back 42 games	inside left 36 games 28 goals	left back 42 games	inside right 41 games 10 goals	centre half 42 games	centre forward 37 games 20 goals	outside left 41 games 10 goals	centre forward 6 games 1 goal

1963–64

Denis Law beats Gordon Banks in the 1963 FA Cup Final

pearances: 22 year old Graham Moore joined from Chelsea in Nov 63, at a cost of £35,000 – but the promise he'd shown as a Welsh cap seemed to evaporate at Old Trafford – and Wilf Tranter, a local lad who'd worked his way

NOEL CANTWELL — left back — 28 games

PAT CRERAND — right half — 41 games — 1 goal

IAN MOIR — winger — 18 games — 3 goals

GEORGE BEST — winger — 17 games — 4 goals

DAVID SADLER — centre forward — 19 games — 5 goals

WILLIE ANDERSON — outside right — 2 games

GRAHAM MOORE — inside right — 18 games — 4 goals — *to Northampton Town 12/65*

WILF TRANTER — centre half — 1 game — *to Brighton and Hove Albion 5/66*

up through the ground staff, managed only one first team game. Also leaving were Phil Chisnall, who wore the United shirt for the first 16 games but then fell from grace, and the ebullient Albert Quixall – after six years, 183 appearances and a total of 56 goals.

The year's three other signings were David Sadler, Willie Anderson and the man Jimmy Greaves would later describe as "the greatest footballer of my lifetime" – George Best. Sadler, who joined from the Isthmian League side Maidstone United, Anderson, a Liverpool kid who signed straight from school, and Best, who joined the United ground staff at 15, all played in the forward line of the youth side which, in 1964, recaptured the FA Youth Cup. All had already made their first team debut – Anderson at 16, Sadler and Best at 17. It was beginning to feel like old times again at Old Trafford... the start of a golden age. Foreseeing this, perhaps, the board of directors arranged for the impressive cantilever stand to be erected – ensuring also that the ground would conform with the specifications for World Cup matches.

The greatest number of spectators ever crammed into Old Trafford was 76,962 – achieved at a 1939 FA Cup game between Wolves and Grimsby. The most who ever watched a United match there was 70,504 – in December 1920, against Aston Villa. By the 63/64 season, attendance fluctuated between 25,848 and 62,965. In March 64, at a sixth round Cup replay against the indefatigable Sunderland at Roker Park, more than 80 fans were injured during scenes more reminiscent of games in the more volatile countries. Some 50,000 were shut out because the ground was full, and punters anxious not to miss the action scaled the roof of the stand and battered down doors. Still, in Lima Peru, two months later, 300 were killed and 1000 injured in a riot during a match against Argentina.

from Burnley in April 64. Already he had ten England caps – and had scored 105 goals for his old club. In his first season with United, he played in every game. What a forward line: Connelly, Charlton, Herd, Law and Best!

NOBBY STILES — left half — 41 games

PAT CRERAND — right half — 39 games — 3 goals

IAN MOIR — outside left — 1 game — *to Blackpool in 2/65*

MAURICE SETTERS — half back — 5 games — *to Stoke City 11/64 for £30,000*

In April 65, Nobby Stiles made his debut for England (against Scotland at Wembley), joining team mate Charlton, who by the end of the season had scored 34 goals for England in 58 matches. There was optimistic speculation about the team's chances in the World Cup next year. Meanwhile, United plunged into Europe again, this time in the Inter Cities Fairs Cup of 1965. In a semi-final play off, they lost out to Ferencvaros, a Hungarian team few people had heard of – but who beat Juventus to take the cup. United also fell in the semi-final of the FA Cup – to Leeds, after a replay. (Leeds lost the final to Liverpool). Nevertheless, the Red Devils of Manchester were back on a roll, playing hugely attractive, reckless, entertaining football. The swinging 60s!

From our Small Acorns dept: history lesson 1: The bizarre details of Manchester United's evolution have been well documented over the years. The roots lie in Newton Heath LYR Football Club, formed by employees of the Lancashire and Yorkshire Railway in 1878. A local pub, The Three Crowns, provided an operational base and a makeshift pitch on recreation grounds in North Road gave them an opportunity to develop. They began to take themselves seriously... who wants to work on the railways if they can make a living playing football? In 1885 they took the plunge and turned professional, later gaining admittance to the Football Alliance – the less prestigious contemporaries of the Football League. In 1892, the Football League absorbed the Alliance and the club became known to all and sundry as Newton Heath.

They entered Football League annals on 3-9-92 with a First Division fixture against Blackburn Rovers, which they lost 3-4... but the following month, their seventh game brought a result which has never been bettered in a hundred years, a 10-1 victory over their perennial rivals Wolverhampton Wanderers. Over the next two years, seesaw fortunes found them ensconced at a new larger capacity ground off Bank Street in Clayton, but relegated to Division Two. A local derby rivalry began in Nov 1894, when they met Manchester City for the first time: Newton Heath came out on top, 5-2. Always veering towards bankruptcy, they eventually croaked within a year of Queen Victoria and would have vanished had not a local brewer, John Davies, financed a metamorphosis. On the 28th April 1902, under his chairmanship, the team re-emerged as... MANCHESTER UNITED.

1964-65

Back Row (l/r)
Jack Crompton, Bill Foulkes, David Sadler, Pat Dunne, Shay Brennan, Graham Moore, Pat Crerand, Noel Cantwell, Matt Busby

Front Row (l/r)
John Connelly, Nobby Stiles, Bobby Charlton, Denis Law, Tony Dunne, David Herd, George Best

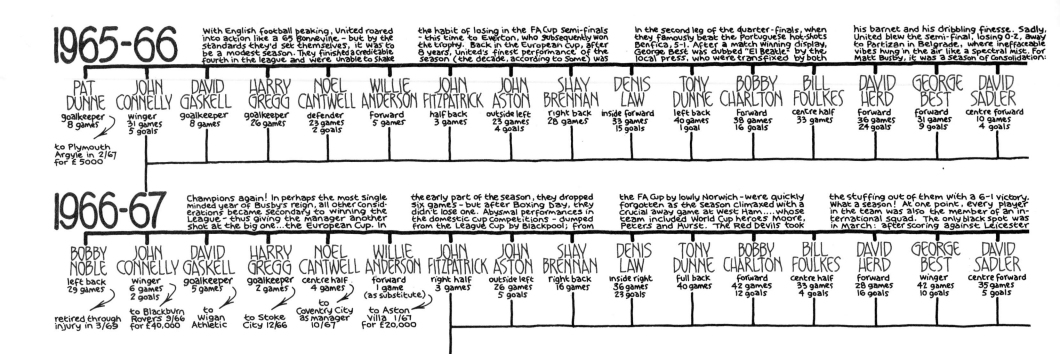

1965-66

With English football peaking, United roared into action like a 65 Bonneville - but by the standards they'd set themselves, it was to be a modest season. They finished a creditable fourth in the league and were unable to shake the habit of losing in the FA Cup Semi-finals - this time to Everton, who subsequently won the trophy. Back in the European Cup, after 8 years, United's finest performance of the season (the decade, according to some) was in the second leg of the quarter-finals, when they famously beat the Portuguese hot-shots Benfica, 5-1. After a match winning display, George Best was dubbed "El Beatle" by the local press, who were transfixed by both his barnet and his dribbling finesse. Sadly, United blew the semi-final, losing 0-2, away to Partizan in Belgrade, where ineffaceable vibes hung in the air like a spectral mist. For Matt Busby, it was a season of consolidation:

PAT DUNNE	JOHN CONNELLY	DAVID GASKELL	HARRY GREGG	NOEL CANTWELL	WILLIE ANDERSON	JOHN FITZPATRICK	JOHN ASTON	SHAY BRENNAN	DENIS LAW	TONY DUNNE	BOBBY CHARLTON	BILL FOULKES	DAVID HERD	GEORGE BEST	DAVID SADLER
goalkeeper 8 games	winger 31 games 5 goals	goalkeeper 8 games	goalkeeper 26 games	defender 23 games 2 goals	forward 5 games	half back 3 games	outside left 23 games 4 goals	right back 28 games	inside forward 33 games 15 goals	left back 40 games 1 goal	forward 38 games 16 goals	centre half 33 games	forward 36 games 24 goals	forward 31 games 9 goals	centre forward 10 games 4 goals

to Plymouth Argyle in 2/67 for £5000

1966-67

Champions again! In perhaps the most single minded year of Busby's reign, all other considerations became secondary to winning the League - thus giving the manager another shot at the big one...the European Cup. In the early part of the season, they dropped six games - but after Boxing Day, they didn't lose one. Abysmal performances in the domestic cup competitions - dumped from the League Cup by Blackpool; from the FA Cup by lowly Norwich - were quickly forgotten as the season climaxed with a crucial away game at West Ham....whose team included World Cup heroes Moore, Peters and Hurst. The Red Devils took the stuffing out of them with a 6-1 victory. What a season! At one point, every player in the team was also the member of an international squad. The only black spot was in March: after scoring against Leicester

BOBBY NOBLE	JOHN CONNELLY	DAVID GASKELL	HARRY GREGG	NOEL CANTWELL	WILLIE ANDERSON	JOHN FITZPATRICK	JOHN ASTON	SHAY BRENNAN	DENIS LAW	TONY DUNNE	BOBBY CHARLTON	BILL FOULKES	DAVID HERD	GEORGE BEST	DAVID SADLER
left back 29 games 2 goals	winger 6 games 2 goals	goalkeeper 5 games	goalkeeper 2 games	centre half 4 games	forward 1 game (as substitute)	right half 3 games	outside left 26 games 5 goals	right back 16 games	inside right 36 games 23 goals	full back 40 games	forward 42 games 12 goals	centre half 33 games 4 goals	forward 28 games 16 goals	winger 42 games 10 goals	centre forward 35 games 5 goals

retired through injury in 3/69 — to Blackburn Rovers 9/66 for £40,000 — to Wigan Athletic — to Stoke City 12/66 — to Coventry City as manager 10/67 — to Aston Villa 1/67 for £20,000

1965–66

Back Row (l/r)
Nobby Stiles, Tony Dunne, David Gaskell, Pat Dunne, Pat Crerand, John Fitzpatrick

Middle Row (l/r)
Jack Crompton, Shay Brennan, David Sadler, Bill Foulkes, John Aston, Noel Cantwell, Matt Busby

Front Row (l/r)
John Connelly, Bobby Charlton, David Herd, Denis Law, George Best

he introduced only two new players to the first eleven – Jimmy Ryan and Bobby Noble, who between them played just six games. The leading scorer, Herd netted goals in the first and last matches, with 22 in between.

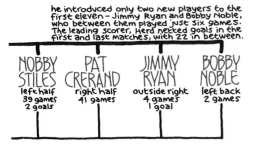

NOBBY STILES	PAT CRERAND	JIMMY RYAN	BOBBY NOBLE
left half 39 games 2 goals	right half 41 games	outside right 4 games 1 goal	left back 2 games

City, last season's leading marksman David Herd was stretchered off with a fractured leg – an injury which was to severely curtail his career. George Best and Bobby Charlton played in every game; Denis Law scored more.

NOBBY STILES	PAT CRERAND	JIMMY RYAN	ALEX STEPNEY
left half 37 games 3 goals	right half 39 games 3 goals	forward 4 games	goalkeeper 35 games

Jimmy Ryan had left school in Stirling to forge a future with United, signing pro at the beginning of 1963. Understudy to the ABC team – Aston, Best and Connelly – he hardly got a look in, poor guy. Bobby Noble, recruited a month earlier, was to face similar problems. A Stockport and Cheshire Schoolboy, he quickly found his way into the England Youth team – but it proved almost impossible to find his way round Noel Cantwell and Tony Dunne. The unrelated Pat Dunne was the only first team player to leave the picture. Quite outstanding the previous season, he found himself cue out of contention during 65/66 – first by Gaskell and then Gregg. After an unconscionably long spell in the reserves, he left to find more of the spotlight on the Devon riviera, keeping goal for Plymouth.

A comprehensive spring-clean saw United reduced to a core of only 14 players – including the year's sole acquisition, goalkeeper Alex Stepney, who made his debut a day before his 24th birthday, in front of 62000 fans packed into Old Trafford to watch the local derby with City. Stepney had made his reputation at Millwall, before being bought by Chelsea for £50,000. Four months later, that club made a quick £5000 profit when he moved on to United, where he would collect a League Championship medal, a European Cup winners medal, and an England cap before the decade was out. Leaving Old Trafford after 9 years and a total of 247 league and cup games was former first-choice goalie, Harry Gregg – one of six players to decamp.

For the first time, teams were allowed to use substitutes during the 65/66 season – and the United player who can claim the distinction of being the first in a number 12 shirt was John Fitzpatrick. He replaced Law at White Hart Lane on 16·10·65, when United were on their way to getting whipped 5-1 by Spurs. During the season, Connelly, Herd and Anderson also made one appearance each from the subs' bench.

For the sake of clarity, unless otherwise noted, the number of games played (as detailed under the players' names) does not include appearances as substitutes, or in any non-League games.

It was in 1966 that the global popularity of football rocketed – thanks to television coverage.

Also on the move were Connelly, Gaskell, Anderson, the old warhorse Cantwell (progressing to management at the hoary age of 35), and – when it became evident that he would never recover full fitness – the promising Bobby Noble, who was only 21 when injuries sustained in a car crash effectively ended his playing career.

The first time police ever used closed circuit television to detect and monitor hooliganism in the crowd at a football match, was at Old Trafford on 10·12·66, during a game against Liverpool. The practice soon grew widespread.

It was in 1967 that Celtic became the first UK team to win the European Cup. Matt Busby doffed his hat to their manager Jock Stein.

Perhaps sensing that they would never get close again, the England team excelled themselves in the 1966 World Cup, the final rounds of which were held on British grounds. In the quarter final between England and Argentina, Rattin – the latter's captain – was sent off and play was held up for seven minutes as his churlish team mates protested. The bemused England side maintained their composure, leaving the field triumphant. Manager Alf Ramsey made pointed remarks about the South Americans' standards of behaviour and FIFA were later to suspend 3 of their players. The final, at Wembley on 30·7·66, was a nail-biter of heroic proportions – with the West Germans equalising 30 seconds before time...after England had led 2-1. In extra time, England scored twice, their final goal coming with the last kick of the match. "They think it's all over," cried the exultant Ken Wolstenholme, as fans invaded the pitch, "...it is now!" And it was. A tick of time to savour. Nobby Stiles played in every World Cup game and won the nation's heart with his one-man conga after the final – but it was Bobby Charlton, at his unruffled best, scoring goals from impossible range and working with ambassadorial grace under pressure, who really shone throughout the tournament. An indication that, with the possible exception of Pelé, he was the most famous footballer in history, came when kids all over the world, whose only previous knowledge of English had been such expressions as "fish and chips" and "Beatles" now added "Bob-bee Charl-ton" to their repertoire. A proud tingle ran down the spine of everyone who loved football when he was voted 1966 European Player Of The Year. What a heady time it was... and though England's subsequent chances were kicked into touch, Manchester United were still on course for that trophy Busby so desperately wanted ...the European Cup.

1966–67

Back Row (l/r)
Shay Brennan, David Gaskell, Nobby Stiles, Bobby Noble, Tony Dunne

Middle Row (l/r)
Jack Crompton, John Aston, David Sadler, Pat Crerand, Alex Stepney, Bill Foulkes, Noel Cantwell

Front Row (l/r)
Jimmy Ryan, George Best, Denis Law, David Herd, Bobby Charlton, John Fitzpatrick

In the aftermath of the Munich crash, Matt Busby was offered the job of manager of Real Madrid by owner Santiago Bernabau. Had he accepted, he would have won the European Cup in 59, 60 and 66 - but he preferred to stay at Old Trafford, believing the only true memorial for the boys who died was a United victory in the world's premier club competition. Everything at the club was geared to that end. And this year it happened. Having shown the door to Hibernians of Malta, FK Sarajevo of Yugoslavia and Gornick Zabrze (who had 105,000 fans through the turnstiles for the game in Poland), United faced a daunting prospect in the semi-final... Real Madrid. 8 times finalists; the fanciest ballplayers in Europe. United won the first leg, at home, 1-0. In Spain, a gate of 125,000 gathered to watch the second leg. Down 3-1 at half time, a resolute United drew level to go through 4-3 on aggregate. The final was at Wembley; the opponents Benfica - a Portuguese team with more European pedigree than Jacques Delors, led by Eusebio, the sensation of the 1966 World Cup. Charlton scored - then Benfica equalised. 1-1 after 90 minutes. In extra time, United nailed Benfica with 3 goals (Best, Charlton and Kidd). Songs of praise, tears of jubilation!

1967-68

European Champions at last! In a career peppered with finest hours, Matt Busby realised a ten year ambition when team captain Bobby Charlton led his boys to glory in the European Cup. Again the concentration was total: the club didn't even enter the League Cup - and they got the distraction of the FA Cup out of the way quickly, losing to Spurs in the third round. They contested the League title

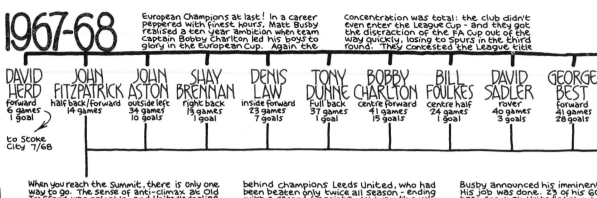

DAVID HERD
forward
6 games
1 goal

to Stoke City 7/68

JOHN FITZPATRICK
half back/forward
14 games

JOHN ASTON
outside left
34 games
10 goals

SHAY BRENNAN
right back
13 games
1 goal

DENIS LAW
inside forward
23 games
7 goals

TONY DUNNE
Full back
37 games
1 goal

BOBBY CHARLTON
centre forward
41 games
15 goals

BILL FOULKES
centre half
24 games
1 goal

DAVID SADLER
rover
40 games
3 goals

GEORGE BEST
forward
41 games
28 goals

In 68/69, the reigning Footballer Of The Year and European Player of The Year, George Best was again United's top goalscorer, bagging 19. (The total was only a measly 54). At 22 years of age, his career was peaking early... too early. Denis Law, still in rumbustious hat-trick form, was celebrated in a new terrace anthem based on the current chart-topper, Lily The Pink:
"We'll drink a drink, a drink
To Denis the King, the King, the King
Cos he's the leader of our football team
He's the greatest centre forward
That the world has ever seen."
No longer Babes, the average age of the team had crept up to 27½. Too much rested on the big name players, whose understudies lacked their lustre.

1968-69

When you reach the summit, there is only one way to go. The sense of anti-climax at Old Trafford was palpable, and United's decline was dramatic. In the league they dropped 10 places, finishing 11th - a full 25 points behind champions Leeds United, who had been beaten only twice all season - ending with a record 67 points. Midway through the season, United had won only 7 of their first 25 games, when - in January - Matt Busby announced his imminent retirement. His job was done. 23 of his 60 years had been spent at United's helm, but though he was stepping aside as manager, letting go of the wheel completely was out of the question.

CARLO SARTORI
midfield
11 games

WILLIE MORGAN
Winger
29 games
6 goals

STEVE JAMES
centre half
21 games
1 goal

JOHN FITZPATRICK
midfield
28 games
3 goals

JOHN ASTON
forward
13 games
2 goals

SHAY BRENNAN
right back
13 games

DENIS LAW
inside forward
30 games
14 goals

TONY DUNNE
left back
33 games

BOBBY CHARLTON
centre forward
32 games
5 goals

BILL FOULKES
centre half
10 games

DAVID SADLER
rover
26 games

GEORGE BEST
forward
41 games
19 goals

1967–68

Back Row (l/r)
Bill Foulkes, John Aston, Jimmy Rimmer, Alex Stepney, Alan Gowling, David Herd

Middle Row (l/r)
David Sadler, Tony Dunne, Shay Brennan, Pat Crerand, George Best, Francis Burns, Jack Crompton

Front Row (l/r)
Jimmy Ryan, Nobby Stiles, Denis Law, Sir Matt Busby, Bobby Charlton, Brian Kidd, John Fitzpatrick

hotly though, eventually coming second to their Maine Road rivals by only 2 thin points. It was a fabulous time to live in 'Manchester: City had their own Best, Law and Charlton in Summerbee, Bell and Lee, and played stunning football. Nevertheless, it was United that most wanted to see: Crowds at Old Trafford averaged 57,000, a league record, and every ground the Reds descended on recorded their highest attendance of the season. Within weeks of the European Cup triumph, Busby was honoured with a knighthood. Sir Matt Busby, Kt, CBE... the proudest man in British football!

George Best, oozing glamour, was now the playboy of the north western world - first choice celebrity for opening boutiques and night clubs - and on the pitch, he was the majestic magician. Reliable too. He played in every game but one, and was the league's top scorer with 28 goals - an unheard number for a winger. To cap the season, he became the third United player (in four years) to be voted European Player Of The Year. With Herd benched and Law frequently injured (he watched the Euro final from his hospital bed), Best found upfront support from two other youth team graduates - John Aston Jr. whose father was now a United coach, and Brian Kidd, 18 years old and in his first season. 15 goals in 38 games...not a bad start. And the best was yet to come: he scored a goal in the European Cup final, which happened to coincide with his 19th birthday. A former Manchester Schoolboy who went pro with United at 17, Kidd was one of 5 new players, all of whom had joined the club straight from school. From Falkirk and Southport respectively, Frank Kopel and Jimmy Rimmer managed only 1 appearance each in 1967-8, but Francis Burns, another young Scot, was given his head early in the season and never looked back. He even got a couple of goals. Alan Gowling could have studied at Cambridge University, but chose instead a course which could accommodate his passion for football. He worked on an economics degree at Manchester University while playing for United's reserves; a ploy which inevitably led to his being known as "Bamber" in the dressing room!

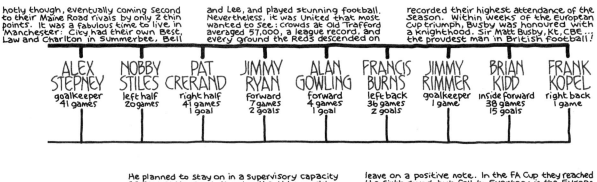

ALEX STEPNEY	NOBBY STILES	PAT CRERAND	JIMMY RYAN	ALAN GOWLING	FRANCIS BURNS	JIMMY RIMMER	BRIAN KIDD	FRANK KOPEL
goalkeeper 41 games	left half 20 games	right half 41 games 1 goal	forward 7 games 2 goals	forward 4 games 1 goal	left back 36 games 2 goals	goalkeeper 1 game	inside forward 38 games 15 goals	right back 1 game

He planned to stay on in a supervisory capacity as General Manager. Knowing they'd be working for a different boss next season - and many of them had never worked for anyone else in their lives - the team rallied to let Sir Matt leave on a positive note. In the FA Cup they reached the Sixth round, but fell to Everton; in the European Cup they often looked as though they might pull it off twice in a row...but ultimately AC Milan got the better of them in a most frustrating semi-final.

In his final acts of refurbishment, Busby drafted in three new boys: Steve James, Willie Morgan and Carlo Sartori. The first Italian-born player to don the red jersey, Sartori had been raised in Collyhurst and represented both Manchester and Lancashire Schoolboys before signing with United on his 17th birthday. James, a Wolverhampton lad, also signed at 17 - earmarked to take over the number 5 shirt from Bill Foulkes. The acquisition of Willie Morgan, secured from Burnley at a cost of £100,000, was Busby's only foray into the fickle transfer market. A Best-alike winger from Alloa, he had a field day when United gave QPR an 8-1 larruping; he netted a hat-trick. However, his seven year stint at Old Trafford was to coincide with a dispiriting period of almost terminal decline in the club's fortunes.

There was an unsavoury coda to the 1968/69 season. In July, after investigations into the rumours surrounding irregular payments to players, United were fined £7000 in a joint FA and Football League Commission. The club was also barred from playing friendly games against any other FA club before May 1970. It was a turning point; the end of a golden era.

Pundits suggested various candidates to take over when Busby vacated his office.... Jimmy Adamson, Dave Sexton and Don Revie among them - but speculation ended when the job was given to Wilf McGuinness, the 31 year old former Busby Babe, who'd been working the back room since a broken leg ended his playing career almost ten years earlier. He succeeded in June 69, initially as Chief Coach.

ALEX STEPNEY	NOBBY STILES	PAT CRERAND	JIMMY RYAN	ALAN GOWLING	FRANCIS BURNS	JIMMY RIMMER	BRIAN KIDD	FRANK KOPEL
goalkeeper 38 games	left half 41 games 1 goal	right half 35 games 1 goal	forward 6 games 1 goal	forward 2 games	left back 14 games	goalkeeper 4 games	inside forward 28 games 1 goal	full back 7 games

to Blackburn Rovers in 3/69 for £25,000

1968–69

Back Row (l/r)
David Sadler, Bill Foulkes, Francis Burns, Bobby Charlton

Middle Row (l/r)
John Fitzpatrick, David Herd, Alex Stepney, Pat Crerand, Nobby Stiles, Jimmy Rimmer, Shay Brennan, Jack Crompton

Front Row (l/r)
Tony Dunne, George Best, Denis Law, Brian Kidd, John Aston

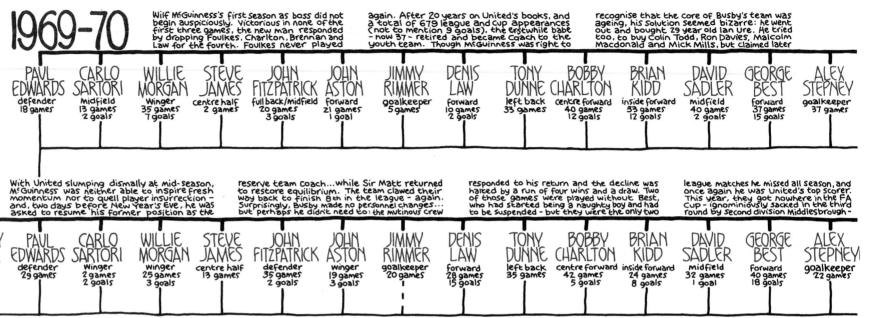

1969-70

During the first half of 1970, Nobby Stiles and Bobby Charlton played their last matches for England. Stiles made his exit in April, after winning 28 caps over 5 years, and Charlton in June – after England were bounced from the World Cup by the West Germans. In a glorious international career spanning 12 years, he won 106 caps. His tally of 49 goals has never been equalled... a hero when the England team were the world's finest.

Wilf McGuinness's first season as boss did not begin auspiciously. Victorious in none of the first three games, the new man responded by dropping Foulkes. Charlton, Brennan and Law for the fourth. Foulkes never played again. After 20 years on United's books, and a total of 679 league and cup appearances (not to mention 9 goals), the erstwhile babe – now 37 – retired and became coach to the youth team. Though McGuinness was right to recognise that the core of Busby's team was ageing, his solution seemed bizarre: he went out and bought 29 year old Ian Ure. He tried too, to buy Colin Todd, Ron Davies, Malcolm Macdonald and Mick Mills, but claimed later

PAUL EDWARDS	CARLO SARTORI	WILLIE MORGAN	STEVE JAMES	JOHN FITZPATRICK	JOHN ASTON	JIMMY RIMMER	DENIS LAW	TONY DUNNE	BOBBY CHARLTON	BRIAN KIDD	DAVID SADLER	GEORGE BEST	ALEX STEPNEY
defender 18 games	midfield 13 games 2 goals	winger 35 games 7 goals	centre half 2 games	full back/midfield 20 games 3 goals	forward 21 games 1 goal	goalkeeper 5 games	forward 10 games 2 goals	left back 33 games	centre forward 40 games 12 goals	inside forward 53 games 12 goals	midfield 40 games 2 goals	forward 37 games 15 goals	goalkeeper 37 games

1970-71

With United slumping dismally at mid-season, McGuinness was neither able to inspire fresh momentum nor to quell player insurrection – and, two days before New Year's Eve, he was asked to resume his former position as the reserve team coach... while Sir Matt returned to restore equilibrium. The team clawed their way back to finish 8th in the league – again. Surprisingly, Busby made no personnel changes... but perhaps he didn't need to: the mutinous crew responded to his return and the decline was halted by a run of four wins and a draw. Two of those games were played without Best, who had started being a naughty boy and had to be suspended – but they were the only two league matches he missed all season, and once again he was United's top scorer. This year, they got nowhere in the FA Cup – ignominiously sacked in the third round by second division Middlesbrough –

WILLIE WATSON	TOMMY O'NEIL	PAUL EDWARDS	CARLO SARTORI	WILLIE MORGAN	STEVE JAMES	JOHN FITZPATRICK	JOHN ASTON	JIMMY RIMMER	DENIS LAW	TONY DUNNE	BOBBY CHARLTON	BRIAN KIDD	DAVID SADLER	GEORGE BEST	ALEX STEPNEY
full back 8 games	full back 1 game	defender 29 games	winger 2 games 2 goals	winger 25 games 3 goals	centre half 13 games	defender 35 games 2 goals	winger 19 games 3 goals	goalkeeper 20 games	forward 28 games 15 goals	left back 35 games	centre forward 42 games 5 goals	inside forward 24 games 8 goals	midfield 32 games 1 goal	forward 40 games 18 goals	goalkeeper 22 games

1969–70

Back Row (l/r)
Don Givens, Ken Goodeve, David Sadler, Alex Stepney, John Connaughton, Jimmy Rimmer, John McInally, Nick Murphy, Jimmy Hall, Alan Gowling

Middle Row (l/r)
Sir Matt Busby, John Aston, Willie Watson, Peter Woods, Jimmy Ryan, Bill Foulkes, Shay Brennan, Bernard Daniels, Brian Kidd, Paul Edwards, Mike Kelly, Wilf McGuinness, Jimmy Murphy

Sitting (l/r)
Jack Crompton, Nobby Stiles, Willie Morgan, Denis Law, Bobby Charlton, Pat Crerand, Tony Dunne, John Aston, Francis Burns

Front Row (l/r)
Carlo Sartori, John Fitzpatrick, Peter O'Sullivan, George Best

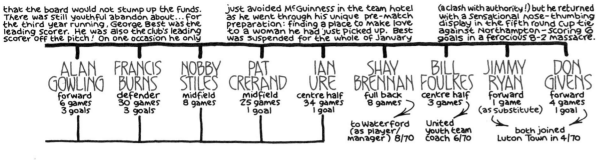

that the board would not stump up the funds. There was still youthful abandon about... For the third year running, George Best was the leading scorer. He was also the club's leading scorer off the pitch! On one occasion he only

just avoided McGuinness in the team hotel as he went through his unique pre-match preparation: finding a place to make love to a woman he had just picked up. Best was suspended for the whole of January

(a clash with authority!) but he returned with a sensational nose-thumbing display in the fifth round Cup tie against Northampton - scoring 6 goals in a ferocious 8-2 massacre.

The season's major procurement, the Scottish international Ian Ure, was a native of Ayr but made his name at Dundee before moving to Arsenal in August 63 for a record transfer fee of £62,500. Six years later, he was Wilf McGuinness's pick to click, a snip at £80,000. Paul Edwards, from the satellite town of Shaw, seized the initiative after an apprenticeship in the reserves, where he had done sterling work since joining the club's professional roster in Feb 65..... but Dubliner Don Givens, another school boy signing, came and went after only a handful of appearances in the red shirt. Ironically, during his short spell at Old Trafford, he represented the Republic of Ireland more than United!

In the 1969/70 season, inconsistent play left United well down the league table, at 8th position - but that was still 3 places higher than last year. Inexplicably, their performances in both the FA Cup and the League Cup were positively astral by comparison. In the former, they stormed to the semi final but Leeds eventually won the day - at the third attempt, 1-0, after two scoreless draws. In the League Cup, they again reached the semi final, only to be vanquished by the Maine Road boys in blue. All things considered, it wasn't a bad year... it was just that United fans had grown accustomed to more. Analysts agreed ...McGuinness didn't have Matt Busby's midas touch. Give the poor guy a chance!

ALAN GOWLING	FRANCIS BURNS	NOBBY STILES	PAT CRERAND	IAN URE	SHAY BRENNAN	BILL FOULKES	JIMMY RYAN	DON GIVENS
forward 6 games 3 goals	defender 30 games 3 goals	midfield 8 games	midfield 25 games 1 goal	centre half 34 games 1 goal	full back 8 games	centre half 3 games	forward 1 game (as substitute)	forward 4 games 1 goal

to Waterford (as player/manager) 8/70

United youth team coach 6/70

both joined Luton Town in 4/70

but reached the semi-final of the League Cup, there falling to Aston Villa. A season best forgotten.... but worse was to come. Those who skipped through the sizzling,

scintillating sixties had no idea just how tacky and tawdry and crappy the seventies would be by comparison. Oh dear!

In a year of tumult, not a bean was spent on new players. The only arrivals were a couple of full backs - Willie Watson from Motherwell and Tommy O'Neil from St Helens — both of whom had followed the traditional amateur, ground staff, signing pro at 17 route... and both of whom were destined for the footnotes of history. O'Neil's debut, in the last game of the season, was exceptional only for an unscheduled appearance on the field by Eamonn Andrews, there to accost Busby with those nerve-wracking words "Sir Matt ...this is your loife." Leaving the club were two stalwarts, Stiles and Crerand, and the recently arrived Ure, who seemed to have run out of steam at Old Trafford. Nobby Stiles, the first United player to have a wax effigy in Madame Tussaud's, was also subjected to the red book treatment on This Is Your Life. One

of Busby's great discoveries, he became one of the best loved stars of British football, his jubilant World Cup victory dance the most enduring snapshot of England's soccer peak. In his 13 year spell at Old Trafford, Stiles logged 392 league and cup appearances - exactly the same total as Paddy Crerand, who played his last games for United during the 1970/71 season and retired not long after the start of the next. Slowly, the old guard was changing. Despite his move upstairs, Busby had remained the same old father figure, maintaining a knack of treating everyone as if they were special, from cleaners to star players; even after retirement, everyone called him "boss". As the season closed, his most urgent task was...find a manager!!

During the 70/71 season, the spotlight was on other teams - especially Arsenal, who beat Liverpool in the FA Cup Final only days after winning the First Division championship, thus becoming the second team in the 20th century to achieve the double. But one United player was seldom out of the news. A trendsetter, jet-setter and trailblazer, George Best represented a new style of footballer. Rather than following tradition with a single-minded devotion to that 90 minute match every week, Best pioneered a new ethic: Look good, kick ass, get laid. Had the description been coined back then, he would have been called an 'alternative' footballer. In the meantime, his more conventional team mates, Brian Kidd (2 caps) and David Sadler (4) played their last England games in 1970.

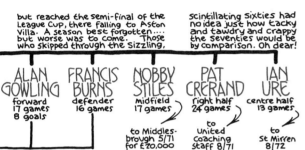

ALAN GOWLING	FRANCIS BURNS	NOBBY STILES	PAT CRERAND	IAN URE
forward 17 games 8 goals	defender 16 games	midfield 17 games	right half 24 games	centre half 13 games

to Middlesbrough 5/71 for £20,000

to United Coaching staff 8/71

to St Mirren 8/72

1970–71

Back Row (l/r)
Paul Edwards, Alan Gowling, David Sadler, John Aston, Brian Kidd, Steve James

Middle Row (l/r)
Jack Crompton, Ian Ure, George Best, Jimmy Rimmer, Alex Stepney, Francis Burns, John Fitzpatrick, Wilf McGuinness, Sir Matt Busby

Front Row (l/r)
Willie Morgan, Tony Dunne, Denis Law, Bobby Charlton, Nobby Stiles, Pat Crerand, Carlo Sartori

1971-72

Charged with finding his successor, Busby failed to land the two men at the top of his shopping list: Jock Stein of Celtic, who initially accepted the offer when the pair met up in a motorway service station and then turned it down after talking to his wife, and Dave Sexton of Chelsea, who wisely waited another six years. The man who landed the job - also after a cuppa on the motorway - was Frank O'Farrell, who had just steered Leicester to promotion from Division Two. He took over on 1st July and United bloomed. Driven by the mercurial Best, who popped in 14 goals during the autumn, and Law, who scored 12, they were five points clear at the top of the table by Christmas. The computer on the BBC's 'Football Focus' predicted that they would win the title by a massive margin. Mystic Meg, eat your heart out! Cracking the champagne prematurely, United suffered a monumental post-Yuletide hangover; seven league matches lost on the

TONY YOUNG	WILLIE WATSON	TOMMY O'NEIL	PAUL EDWARDS	WILLIE MORGAN	STEVE JAMES	JOHN FITZPATRICK	BOBBY CHARLTON	JIMMY RIMMER	DENIS LAW	TONY DUNNE	IAN STOREY-MOORE	BRIAN KIDD	DAVID SADLER	GEORGE BEST	ALEX STEPNEY
midfield	full back	full back	defender	Winger	centre half	full back	centre forward	goalkeeper	forward	full back	forward	forward	midfield	forward	goalkeeper
5 games	0 games	37 games	4 games	35 games 1 goal	37 games 1 goal	1 game	40 games 8 goals	0 games	32 games 13 goals	34 games	11 games 5 goals	34 games 10 goals	37 games 1 goal	40 games 18 goals	39 games

1972-73

Like McGuinness, O'Farrell got his marching orders after 18 months of mediocre match results. The mild, genial Irishman must have wondered what he'd let himself in for! An atmosphere of chaos prevailed, camps had developed, unity crumbled. Best, nobbled by extra-curricular excess, was on the transfer list - with no takers; only three of the first 18 games were won; they'd been booted out of the League Cup by Bristol Rovers and were about to lose the third round of the FA Cup to Wolves; they were languishing at the bottom of Division One. 'How are the mighty fallen' ran the media mockery. Senior players were openly critical of O'Farrell's management, especially his panic buys: Ted MacDougall from Bournemouth for £200,000 - a record for a Division Three man - and Wyn Davies from Manchester City for £25,000. Neither found a welcome in a club on the verge of civil war and neither hung around for more

TED MacDOUGALL	WYN DAVIES	IAN DONALD	WILLIE WATSON	TOMMY O'NEIL	PAUL EDWARDS	JOHN FITZPATRICK	BOBBY CHARLTON	JIMMY RIMMER	DENIS LAW	TONY DUNNE	IAN STOREY-MOORE	BRIAN KIDD	DAVID SADLER	GEORGE BEST	ALEX STEPNEY
Forward	forward	Full back	full back	full back	defender	midfield	centre forward	goalkeeper	forward	full back	forward	forward	Midfield	forward	goalkeeper
18 games 5 goals	15 games 4 goals	4 games	3 games	16 games	1 game	5 games	34 games 6 goals	4 games	9 games 1 goal	24 games	26 games 5 goals	17 games 4 goals	19 games	19 games 4 goals	38 games
to West Ham Utd in 3/73	to Blackpool in 6/73	to Partick Thistle 1/73	to Miami Toros 5/73	to Southport in 8/73	to Oldham Ath 3/73	quit football in 7/73	to Preston as manager in 5/73	to Arsenal in 4/74 for £40,000	to Manchester City in 7/73	to Bolton Wanderers in 8/73					

1971–72

Back Row (l/r)
John Fitzpatrick, Alan Gowling, Paul Edwards, Steve James, Jimmy Rimmer, Alex Stepney, Ian Ure, David Sadler, Tony Dunne, Bobby Charlton

Front Row (l/r)
Francis Burns, Brian Kidd, George Best, Denis Law, Pat Crerand, Willie Morgan, John Aston, Carlo Sartori

trot. Whoops! A stunned O'Farrell moved into the transfer market, buying two high-coin players, Ian Storey-Moore and Martin Buchan. A former Scottish Player of the Year and regular Scottish international, Buchan cost £125,000

when he moved down from Aberdeen to spend eleven years at Old Trafford – six as captain. Notts Forest were paid £200,000 for their leading goalscorer, Storey-Moore, who promptly arrested the decline by scoring in his first three matches with United.

A prosaic FA Cup run ended at round 6, when Stoke took them out – having also removed them from the League Cup a little earlier. In Division One, they finished 8th – for the third year running. O'Farrell discussed their

shortcomings with Busby, who had now given up the title of General Manager in favour of joining the board. He still kept an office at Old Trafford, however, and came into work every day as before. Old customs die hard.

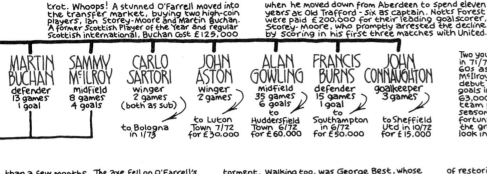

MARTIN BUCHAN — defender — 13 games — 1 goal

SAMMY McILROY — midfield — 8 games — 4 goals

CARLO SARTORI — winger — 2 games (both as sub) — to Bologna in 1/73

JOHN ASTON — winger — 2 games — to Luton Town 7/72 for £30,000

ALAN GOWLING — midfield — 35 games — 6 goals — to Huddersfield Town 6/72 for £60,000

FRANCIS BURNS — defender — 15 games — 1 goal — to Southampton in 6/72 for £50,000

JOHN CONNAUGHTON — goalkeeper — 3 games — to Sheffield Utd in 10/72 for £15,000

Two youngsters got their first taste of the big time in 71/72, having been taken on by Busby in the late 60s as school leavers. A Belfast boy, Sammy McIlroy floated trance-like off the field after his debut at Maine Road, where he scored one of the goals in an explosive local derby – attended by over 63,000. Tony Young, from Urmston, gained first team promotion only in the last month of the season – but immediately looked promising. Less fortunate was John Connaughton, who had joined the ground staff in January 65, but hardly got a look in. He was one of 5 players on the move.

The flickeringly brilliant George Best, who'd scored 14 goals, including two hat-tricks, before the end of November, managed only 4 more all season – but he was still top scorer for the umpteenth consecutive year. His form dipped after an IRA death threat (a genuine one; his sister was shot in the leg back home) and unable to cope with mounting pressure, he took to the bottle. He missed training sessions, caroused to the hilt, had wages docked for indiscipline, and caused friction among the other players. At the season's end, he flew to Spain and announced the first of several retirements. It was Busby who persuaded him back.

than a few months. The axe fell on O'Farrell's neck a few days before Christmas, just after a 5-0 humiliation at Crystal Palace. His Xmas box, a 45 grand pay-off, was conditional on his not disclosing any details of his Old Trafford

torment. Walking too, was George Best, whose contract was terminated "by mutual agreement." He went off to toast his new-found freedom. What now? Tommy Docherty, that's what. Thrilled to accept the tough challenge

of restoring United's reputation and self respect, the uncompromising Scot came in with his claymore swishing: "My job was to chop, chop, chop!" Under his ruthless glare, Charlton, Law, Dunne, Edwards, Fitzpatrick, Rimmer, MacDougall, Watson, Donald,

Davies and O'Neil all played their last games for United. Within a month of taking up his new post, Docherty had spent over half a million pounds on new players and a Spring revival saw them clamber out of the relegation zone to finish in 18th place.

MARTIN BUCHAN — defender — 42 games

SAMMY McILROY — midfield — 4 games

TONY YOUNG — defender — 28 games

WILLIE MORGAN — winger — 39 games — 3 goals

STEVE JAMES — defender — 22 games

TREVOR ANDERSON — forward — 2 games — 1 goal

MICK MARTIN — midfield — 14 games — 2 goals

GEORGE GRAHAM — midfield — 18 games — 1 goal

JIM HOLTON — centre back — 15 games — 3 goals

ARNIE SIDEBOTTOM — centre back — 2 games

LOU MACARI — forward — 16 games — 5 goals

ALEX FORSYTH — full back — 8 games

Tragically, United's most illustrious and gifted players, Bobby Charlton & Denis Law, made their exit after a season of undignified backstage intrigues at Old Trafford, and the team's worst performance for a decade. Nobody has come near Charlton's astonishing record of 752 league and cup games – nor his incredible total of 247 goals. Law still lies in second place as a goal-scorer: 236 goals in 393 games. The heart and soul of the great 60s team.

1972–73

Back Row (l/r)
Tommy Cavanagh, Tommy Docherty, David Sadler, Denis Law, Jim Holton, Alex Stepney, Mick Martin, George Graham, Wyn Davies, Alex Forsyth, Martin Buchan, Pat Crerand

Front Row (l/r)
Willie Morgan, Ted MacDougall, Tony Young, Bobby Charlton, Lou Macari, Brian Kidd, Ian Storey-Moore

As soon as he took over in December 72, Tommy Docherty gave United a transfusion. The blood was exclusively Celtic: 80% Scottish/20% Irish... no bias there, then. George Graham cost £120,000 from Arsenal; Lou Macari cost £200,000 when he left Celtic; Alex Forsyth was a £100,000 purchase from Partick Thistle; Jim Holton cost £80,000 from Shrewsbury Town; and Mick Martin was a £25,000 snip from Dublin Bohemians. Three other players debuted during Docherty's first season. Ian Donald from Aberdeen and Arnie Sidebottom from Barnsley had joined United from school. The former returned to Scotland; the latter would ultimately find more acclaim on the cricket field. Trevor Anderson was an O'Farrell innovation, having moved from Portadown at a cost of £20,000. He got short shrift under Docherty, though he was capped six times by Northern Ireland while with United.

During the 73/74 season, Docherty wrought more swingeing changes. In came another 3 Celts: Scotsmen Stewart Houston (who Docherty had signed to Chelsea as an 18 year old and now acquired from Brentford at a cost of £55,000) and Jim McCalliog (who joined from Wolves near the season's end), and future Republic of Ireland Cap Gerry Daly, a £20,000 bargain from Bohemians of Dublin. Also gaining promotion from youth and reserve teams were players who'd signed straight from school: Clive Griffiths, Peter Fletcher, Paul Bielby – none of whom lasted beyond the season – and Brian Greenhoff, a Barnsley boy, who hung on in there. Out went Trevor Anderson, George Best, Ian Storey-Moore, David Sadler and Brian Kidd... but Tommy Docherty survived the 18 month watershed.

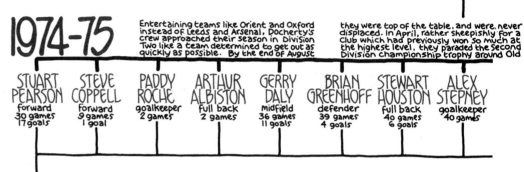

1973-74

The most humiliating season in United's history! Knocked out of both cups early and at home, they were finally – after a couple of years of trying – relegated to Division Two. Had sponsorship been around, the most appropriate word for the front of their shirts would have been BLUNT. It was the forwards who let the side down; at the back, the defence was secure....only 48 goals were conceded – the best since they

PETER FLETCHER	CLIVE GRIFFITHS	PAUL BIELBY	TREVOR ANDERSON	IAN STOREY-MOORE	BRIAN KIDD	DAVID SADLER	GEORGE BEST	ALEX STEPNEY
Forward 2 games	defender 7 games	Forward 2 games	Forward 11 games 1 goal	Forward 2 games 1 goal	Forward 21 games 2 goals	Midfield 2 games	Forward 12 games 2 goals	goalkeeper 42 games 2 goals
to Hull City in 5/73 for £30,000	to Plymouth Argyle (on loan) 7/74	Hartlepool United 12/75	to Swindon Town 11/74	retired on medical advice 12/73	to Arsenal in 8/74 for £110,000	to Preston in 11/73 for £25,000	to Dunstable Town 7/74	

Hooliganism had started to become a real problem in English football, and United were not immune. At the start of the 71/72 season, they had been forced by the FA to close Old Trafford for the first 2 home games following the discovery of a flick knife on the pitch the previous year. Now, after the pitch invasion at the United-City match, where 37 fans had been arrested, the FA disciplinary commission had ordered crowd control fences to be erected at Old Trafford. Undeterred by these offstage distractions, Docherty continued his team renovation. Two key signings bolstered the front line...the 25 year old Stuart Pearson, an armour piercing centre forward, was purchased from Hull City for £200,000 and scored 17 goals in his first season, and Steve Coppell, a 19 year old Liverpool University science student who moonlighted as a frisky winger for Tranmere Rovers joined for £60,000 - in time to wear the number 7 shirt for United's last

games in Division Two. Docherty's most eccentric move was buying the 32 year old Welsh international Ron Davies. A voracious goalscorer for Southampton, he was drafted in at a cost of £25,000 - to languish on the subs' bench. Reserve goalie Paddy Roche, who'd joined from Dublin Shelbourne for £15,000 in October 73, got a lenient first team baptism, and Edinburgh born apprentice Arthur Albiston, a pro at 17, played the first of 464 games for United. Also making two cameo appearances was Tommy Baldwin, on short term loan from Millwall. Meanwhile, Docherty waved goodbye to a string of supernumaries: Morgan, James, McCalliog, Graham, Holton, Martin and Sidebottom. If your face didn't fit, it was game over. Glad to be out of the spotlight, George Best was enjoying life. His name has since become synonymous with squandered talent – although statistics refute that: a total of 466 appearances and 176 goals. "We had our problems with the wee fellow, but I prefer to remember the genius" said Matt Busby.

1974-75

Entertaining teams like Orient and Oxford instead of Leeds and Arsenal, Docherty's crew approached their season in Division Two like a team determined to get out as quickly as possible. By the end of August they were top of the table, and were never displaced. In April, rather sheepishly for a club which had previously won so much at the highest level, they paraded the Second Division championship trophy around Old

STUART PEARSON	STEVE COPPELL	PADDY ROCHE	ARTHUR ALBISTON	GERRY DALY	BRIAN GREENHOFF	STEWART HOUSTON	ALEX STEPNEY
forward 30 games 17 goals	forward 9 games 1 goal	goalkeeper 2 games	full back 2 games	midfield 36 games 11 goals	defender 39 games 4 goals	full back 40 games 6 goals	goalkeeper 40 games

1973–74

Back Row (l/r)
Arnie Sidebottom, Steve James, Alex Stepney, Jimmy Rimmer, Jim Holton, Peter Fletcher

Middle Row (l/r)
Sammy McIlroy, Ian Storey-Moore, Trevor Anderson, Alex Forsyth, Mick Martin, Martin Buchan

Front Row (l/r)
Willie Morgan, Tony Young, Lou Macari, George Graham, Gerry Daly, Brian Kidd, Ray O'Brien

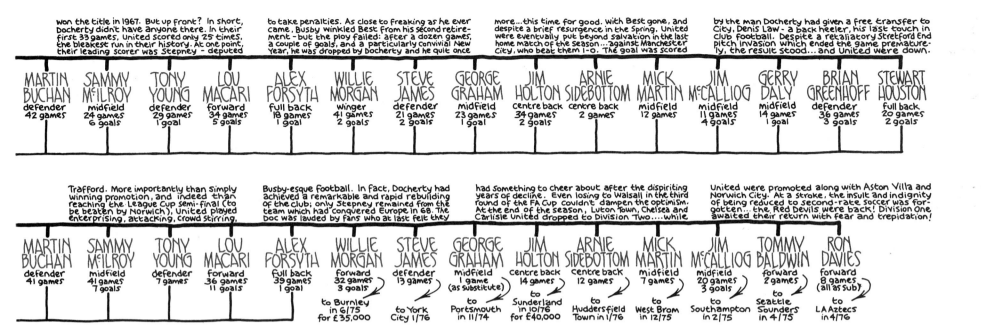

won the title in 1967. But up front? In short, Docherty didn't have anyone there. In their first 33 games, United scored only 25 times, the bleakest run in their history. At one point, their leading scorer was Stepney – deputed

to take penalties. As close to freaking as he ever came. Busby winkled Best from his second retirement – but the ploy failed: after a dozen games, a couple of goals, and a particularly convivial New Year, he was dropped by Docherty and he quit once

more...this time for good. With Best gone, and despite a brief resurgence in the Spring, United were eventually put beyond salvation in the last home match of the season...against Manchester City, who beat them 1-0. The goal was scored

by the man Docherty had given a free transfer to City, Denis Law - a back heeler, his last touch in club football. Despite a retaliatory Stretford End pitch invasion which ended the game prematurely, the result stood... and United were down.

MARTIN BUCHAN	SAMMY McILROY	TONY YOUNG	LOU MACARI	ALEX FORSYTH	WILLIE MORGAN	STEVE JAMES	GEORGE GRAHAM	JIM HOLTON	ARNIE SIDEBOTTOM	MICK MARTIN	JIM McCALLIOG	GERRY DALY	BRIAN GREENHOFF	STEWART HOUSTON
defender 42 games	midfield 24 games 6 goals	defender 29 games 1 goal	forward 34 games 5 goals	full back 18 games 1 goal	winger 41 games 2 goals	defender 21 games 2 goals	midfield 23 games 1 goal	centre back 34 games 2 goals	centre back 2 games	midfield 12 games	midfield 11 games 4 goals	midfield 14 games 1 goal	defender 36 games 3 goals	full back 20 games 2 goals

Trafford. More importantly than simply winning promotion, and indeed more than reaching the League Cup semi-final (to be beaten by Norwich), United played enterprising, attacking, crowd stirring,

Busby-esque football. In fact, Docherty had achieved a remarkable and rapid rebuilding of the club; only Stepney remained from the team which had conquered Europe in 68. The Doc was lauded by fans who at last felt they

had something to cheer about after the dispiriting years of decline. Even losing to Walsall in the third round of the FA Cup couldn't dampen the optimism. At the end of the season, Luton Town, Chelsea and Carlisle United dropped to Division Two....while

United were promoted along with Aston Villa and Norwich City. At a stroke, the insult and indignity of being reduced to second-rate soccer was forgotten... the Red Devils were back! Division One awaited their return with fear and trepidation!

MARTIN BUCHAN	SAMMY McILROY	TONY YOUNG	LOU MACARI	ALEX FORSYTH	WILLIE MORGAN	STEVE JAMES	GEORGE GRAHAM	JIM HOLTON	ARNIE SIDEBOTTOM	MICK MARTIN	JIM McCALLIOG	TOMMY BALDWIN	RON DAVIES
defender 41 games	midfield 41 games 7 goals	defender 7 games	forward 36 games 11 goals	full back 39 games 1 goal	forward 32 games 3 goals → to Burnley in 6/75 for £35,000	defender 13 games → to York City 1/76	midfield 1 game (as substitute) → to Portsmouth in 11/74	centre back 14 games → to Sunderland in 10/76 for £40,000	centre back 12 games → to Huddersfield Town in 1/76	midfield 7 games → to West Brom in 12/75	midfield 20 games 3 goals → to Southampton in 2/75	forward 2 games → to Seattle Sounders in 4/75	forward 8 games (all as sub) → to L A Aztecs in 4/76

1974–75

Back Row (l/r)
Tommy Cavanagh, Jimmy Nicholl, Alan Kirkup, Arnie Sidebottom, Paul Bielby, Jimmy Kelly, Arthur Albiston, Tony Young

Middle Row (l/r)
Tommy Docherty, Lindsey McKeown, George Buchan, Steve James, Paddy Roche, Alex Stepney, Stewart Houston, Martin Buchan, George Graham, Laurie Brown, Jack Crompton, Pat Crerand

Front Row (l/r)
Stuart Pearson, Brian Greenhoff, Jim McCalliog, Sammy McIlroy, Alex Forsyth, Mick Martin, Gerry Daly, Lou Macari, Trevor Anderson

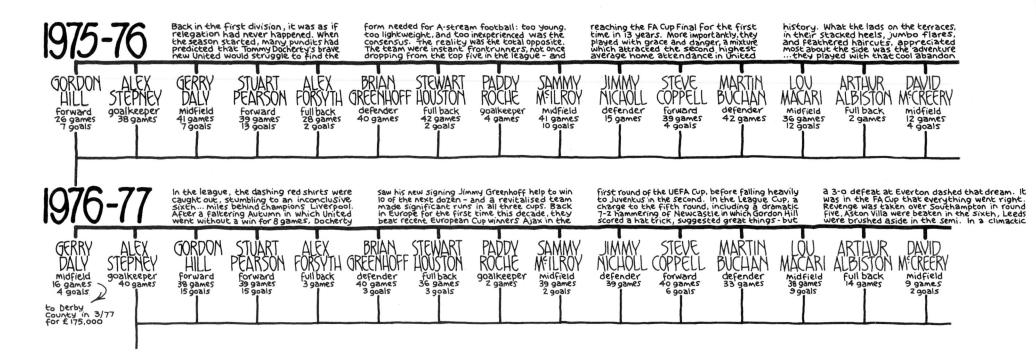

1975-76

Back in the first division, it was as if relegation had never happened. When the season started, many pundits had predicted that Tommy Docherty's brave new United would struggle to find the form needed for A-stream football: too young, too lightweight, and too inexperienced was the consensus. The reality was the total opposite. The team were instant frontrunners, not once dropping from the top five in the league – and reaching the FA Cup Final for the first time in 13 years. More importantly, they played with grace and danger, a mixture which attracted the second highest average home attendance in United history. What the lads on the terraces, in their stacked heels, jumbo flares, and feathered haircuts, appreciated most about the side was the adventure ...they played with that cool abandon

GORDON HILL	ALEX STEPNEY	GERRY DALY	STUART PEARSON	ALEX FORSYTH	BRIAN GREENHOFF	STEWART HOUSTON	PADDY ROCHE	SAMMY McILROY	JIMMY NICHOLL	STEVE COPPELL	MARTIN BUCHAN	LOU MACARI	ARTHUR ALBISTON	DAVID McCREERY
Forward	goalkeeper	midfield	Forward	full back	defender	full back	goalkeeper	midfield	defender	forward	defender	midfield	Full back	midfield
26 games	38 games	41 games	39 games	28 games	40 games	42 games	4 games	41 games	15 games	39 games	42 games	36 games	2 games	12 games
7 goals		7 goals	13 goals	2 goals		2 goals		10 goals		4 goals		12 goals		4 goals

1976-77

In the league, the dashing red shirts were caught out, stumbling to an inconclusive sixth... miles behind champions Liverpool. After a faltering Autumn in which United went without a win for 8 games, Docherty saw his new signing Jimmy Greenhoff help to win 10 of the next dozen – and a revitalised team made significant runs in all three cups. Back in Europe for the first time this decade, they beat recent European Cup winners Ajax in the first round of the UEFA Cup, before falling heavily to Juventus in the second. In the League Cup, a charge to the fifth round, including a dramatic 7-2 hammering of Newcastle in which Gordon Hill scored a hat trick, suggested great things - but a 3-0 defeat at Everton dashed that dream. It was in the FA Cup that everything went right. Revenge was taken over Southampton in round five, Aston Villa were beaten in the sixth, Leeds were brushed aside in the semi. In a climactic

GERRY DALY	ALEX STEPNEY	GORDON HILL	STUART PEARSON	ALEX FORSYTH	BRIAN GREENHOFF	STEWART HOUSTON	PADDY ROCHE	SAMMY McILROY	JIMMY NICHOLL	STEVE COPPELL	MARTIN BUCHAN	LOU MACARI	ARTHUR ALBISTON	DAVID McCREERY
midfield	goalkeeper	forward	forward	full back	defender	full back	goalkeeper	midfield	defender	forward	defender	midfield	full back	midfield
16 games	40 games	38 games	39 games	3 games	40 games	36 games	2 games	39 games	39 games	40 games	33 games	38 games	14 games	9 games
4 goals		15 goals	15 goals		3 goals	3 goals		2 goals		6 goals		9 goals		2 goals

to Derby County in 3/77 for £175,000

1975–76

Back Row (l/r)
Arthur Albiston, Stewart Houston, Alex Stepney, Jim Holton, Paddy Roche, Jimmy Nicholl

Middle Row (l/r)
Tommy Cavanagh, Peter Loughnane, David McCreery, Gordon Hill, Tommy Jackson, Stuart Pearson, Brian Greenhoff, Tommy Docherty, Laurie Brown

Front Row (l/r)
Jim Kelly, Alex Forsyth, Lou Macari, Martin Buchan, Sammy McIlroy, Gerry Daly, Steve Paterson.

Steve Coppell was an unavoidable absentee because of university studies

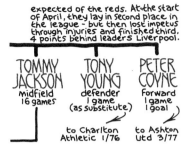

expected of the reds. At the start of April, they lay in second place in the league - but then lost impetus through injuries and finished third, 4 points behind leaders Liverpool.

TOMMY JACKSON
midfield
16 games

TONY YOUNG
defender
1 game
(as substitute)
→ to Charlton Athletic 1/76

PETER COYNE
forward
1 game
1 goal
→ to Ashton Utd 3/77

In the FA Cup, United appeared to be going all the way. A glorious run, which included a 3-2 away victory in the sixth round replay against Wolves, saw them drawn against Derby in the semi-final. Gordon Hill scored both goals in a 2-0 pasting of the club which had topped the league table twice in the previous four years, signalling a change in the order of things. The Gary Glitter-inspired chant from the terraces said it all: "Hello Hello, United are back!" Alas, the final did not go according to the script. In a Wembley overwhelmed by the red horde, the Doc's protégés finally fulfilled those Jeremiahs' predictions made at the start of the season: they froze in the big time. Second division Southampton, shrewdly prepared by Lawrie McMenemy, won 1-0. The goal was scored by Bobby Stokes, so far offside he was practically in Watford, latching onto a pass from a recent Docherty discard, Jim McCalliog!

After a fleeting appearance as United's goalkeeper in 1934, Billy Behan carved a niche as the club's principal Irish talent scout, alerting successive managers to a string of potential stars, the latest of which was David McCreery, who left Belfast for Old Trafford at 15, and worked his way up to first team status two years later. Also making their league debuts during the 75/76 season were Tommy Jackson, Gordon Hill and Jimmy Nicholl. Another Belfast boy, the experienced Northern Ireland international Jackson had played for both Everton and Notts Forest before moving to United, ostensibly to captain the reserve team. Hill was acquired from Millwall at a cost of £70,000 - plus a further £10,000 payable when he won his first England cap. Known as 'Merlin' he played opposite Coppell to mastermind a formidable twin-pronged flank attack - feeding the season's top goal scorers, Pearson and Macari. Nicholl had been born in Canada and raised in Belfast. Joining United from School, he paid his dues as youth team skipper.

History lesson 2: Under John Davies' chairmanship/patronage, Newton Heath FC became Manchester United FC in 1902 - when they switched from blue & white to a red & white strip....the first of many Red Devil designs. It was the dapper Ernest Mangnall, appointed manager in 1903, who first instilled the determination and ambition which have characterised the club for almost a century. At the end of the 1905/06 season, they won promotion to Division One and were attracting crowds of over 15,000. Players like Charlie Roberts, George Wall and Sandy Turnbull became local heroes - none more acclaimed than the dashing winger Billy Meredith, who joined from Manchester City. United won the League Championship for the first time in 1907/8, and the following year won the FA Cup- beating Bristol City 1-0 at The Crystal Palace. In February 1910, the club relocated - to Old Trafford, a purpose built, state of the art stadium bankrolled by proud Chairman Davies. They topped the league again at the end of the 1910/11 season but were relegated to Division Two in 1921/22. Promoted in 1924/25; demoted again in 1930/31; promoted in 1935/36; demoted in 1936/37; promoted in 1937/38! Then the war.

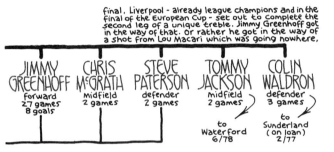

final, Liverpool - already league champions and in the final of the European Cup - set out to complete the second leg of a unique treble. Jimmy Greenhoff got in the way of that. Or rather he got in the way of a shot from Lou Macari which was going nowhere,

JIMMY GREENHOFF
forward
27 games
8 goals

CHRIS McGRATH
midfield
2 games

STEVE PATERSON
defender
2 games

TOMMY JACKSON
midfield
2 games
→ to Waterford 6/78

COLIN WALDRON
defender
3 games
→ to Sunderland (on loan) 2/77

until it struck him on the chest and ballooned comically into the net for the winner in a 2-1 thriller. It was a cruel way for Liverpool to be denied their place in history (they won the European Cup four days later), but few at Old Trafford were too down-hearted about losing out to United. In his speech at last year's post-final dinner, Docherty had urged players and fans not to be too down-hearted about losing out to Southampton: "we'll be back at Wembley next year" he said, "and this time we'll win!"... and now his prediction had come true. Glasses were raised: United were on the come-back trail with their first trophy since the European Cup in 1968. Not for 14 years had they danced round Wembley as FA Cup Final victors. For Docherty particularly, it was a moment to savour...he looked set to lead the club into a new Busby-esque epoch of accomplishment.

Though no-one had any inkling at the time, Jimmy Greenhoff would be Tommy Docherty's last major signing. The older brother (by almost 7 years) of United stalwart Brian, 30 year old Jimmy had already enjoyed fame and fortune as a hot-shot goal scorer at Stoke City, who let him go for a £120,000 transfer fee. His arrival had a marked effect on the team but unfortunately precipitated the departure of crowd favourite Gerry Daly. Not the first player to clash with Docherty, he jumped ship and joined Derby County - ironically, it would transpire. Also making their United debuts during the 76/77 season were Chris McGrath, a Northern Ireland international who cost Docherty £30,000 when he left Spurs, and Steve Paterson, a rugged Scot who had been on the books since the age of 16. The fourth newcomer was former Chelsea and Burnley defender Colin Waldron. Despite over 300 games for Burnley, he found no niche with United.

A month after capering round Wembley with the lid of the FA Cup on his head, Tommy Docherty held an impromptu press conference. In order to pre-empt exposure by a tabloid newspaper he was forced to admit that he had left his wife Agnes to set up home with Mary Brown - the wife of United physiotherapist Laurie Brown. A month later, on 4th July 1977, chairman Louis Edwards called a press conference of his own. Put in an impossible position by an emotional dispute between two employees who could obviously work together no longer, the board decided to back the wronged man. Brown would stay, Docherty was sacked. He left to manage Derby County (re-uniting with Gerry daly) but stayed only until May 79. In a succession of jobs ("I've had more clubs than Jack Nicklaus!" was his standard joke), Docherty never won anything again. Now entertains as an after dinner speaker.

1976–77

Back Row (l/r)
Tommy Cavanagh, Arthur Albiston, Colin Waldron, Paddy Roche, Alex Stepney, Steve Paterson, Jimmy Nicholl, Laurie Brown

Middle Row (l/r)
Tommy Docherty, Alex Forsyth, Brian Greenhoff, Gerry Daly, Ray Storey, Tommy Jackson, David McCreery, Frank Blunstone

Front Row (l/r)
Stuart Pearson, Steve Coppell, Lou Macari, Martin Buchan, Sammy McIlroy, Stewart Houston

INSET
Left: Gordon Hill *Right:* Jimmy Greenhoff

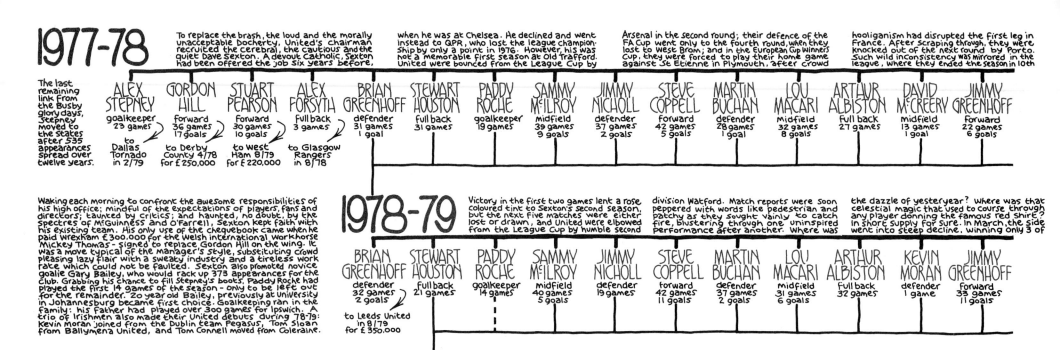

1977-78

To replace the brash, the loud and the morally unacceptable Docherty, United's chairman recruited the cerebral, the cautious and the quiet Dave Sexton. A devout Catholic, Sexton had been offered the job six years before, when he was at Chelsea. He declined and went instead to QPR, who lost the league championship by only a point in 1976. However, his was not a memorable first season at Old Trafford. United were bounced from the League Cup by Arsenal in the second round; their defence of the FA Cup went only to the fourth round, when they lost to West Brom; and in the European Cup Winners Cup, they were forced to play their home game against St Etienne in Plymouth, after crowd hooliganism had disrupted the first leg in France. After scraping through, they were knocked out of the next round by Porto. Such wild inconsistency was mirrored in the league, where they ended the season in 10th

The last remaining link from the Busby glory days, Stepney moved to the states after 535 appearances spread over twelve years.

ALEX STEPNEY goalkeeper 23 games — to Dallas Tornado in 2/79

GORDON HILL forward 36 games 17 goals — to Derby County 4/78 for £250,000

STUART PEARSON forward 30 games 10 goals — to West Ham 8/79 for £220,000

ALEX FORSYTH full back 3 games — to Glasgow Rangers in 8/78

BRIAN GREENHOFF defender 31 games 1 goal

STEWART HOUSTON full back 31 games

PADDY ROCHE goalkeeper 19 games

SAMMY McILROY midfield 39 games 9 goals

JIMMY NICHOLL defender 37 games 2 goals

STEVE COPPELL forward 42 games 5 goals

MARTIN BUCHAN defender 28 games 1 goal

LOU MACARI midfield 32 games 8 goals

ARTHUR ALBISTON full back 27 games

DAVID McCREERY midfield 13 games 1 goal

JIMMY GREENHOFF forward 22 games 6 goals

1978-79

Waking each morning to confront the awesome responsibilities of his high office; mindful of the expectations of players, fans and directors; taunted by critics; and haunted, no doubt, by the spectres of McGuinness and O'Farrell, Sexton kept faith with his existing team. His only use of the chequebook came when he paid Wrexham £300,000 for the Welsh international workhorse Mickey Thomas - signed to replace Gordon Hill on the wing. It was a move typical of the manager's style, substituting crowd pleasing lazy flair with a sweaty industry and a tireless work rate which could not be faulted. Sexton also promoted novice goalie Gary Bailey, who would rack up 373 appearances for the club. Grabbing his chance to fill Stepney's boots, Paddy Roche had played the first 14 games of the season - only to be left out for the remainder. 20 year old Bailey, previously at University in Johannesburg, became first choice. Goalkeeping ran in the family: his father had played over 300 games for Ipswich. A trio of Irishmen also made their United debuts during 78-79: Kevin Moran joined from the Dublin team Pegasus, Tom Sloan from Ballymena United, and Tom Connell moved from Coleraine.

Victory in the first two games lent a rose coloured tint to Sexton's second season, but the next five matches were either lost or drawn, and United were elbowed from the League Cup by humble second division Watford. Match reports were soon peppered with words like pedestrian and patchy as they sought vainly to catch fire, blustering through one uninspired performance after another. Where was the dazzle of yesteryear? Where was that celestial magic that used to course through any player donning the famous red shirt? In short supply for sure. In March, the side went into steep decline, winning only 3 of

BRIAN GREENHOFF defender 32 games 2 goals — to Leeds United in 8/79 for £350,000

STEWART HOUSTON full back 21 games

PADDY ROCHE goalkeeper 14 games

SAMMY McILROY midfield 40 games 5 goals

JIMMY NICHOLL defender 19 games

STEVE COPPELL forward 42 games 11 goals

MARTIN BUCHAN defender 37 games 2 goals

LOU MACARI midfield 31 games 6 goals

ARTHUR ALBISTON full back 32 games

KEVIN MORAN defender 1 game

JIMMY GREENHOFF forward 33 games 11 goals

1977–78

Back Row (l/r)
Tommy Cavanagh, Arthur Albiston, Alex Forsyth, Jimmy Nicholl, Brian Greenhoff, Paddy Roche, Stewart Houston, Alex Stepney, Gordon McQueen, Ashley Grimes, Tommy Jackson, Dave Sexton

Front Row (l/r)
Steve Coppell, David McCreery, Chris McGrath, Lou Macari, Martin Buchan, Joe Jordan, Stuart Pearson, Jimmy Greenhoff, Sammy McIlroy, Laurie Brown

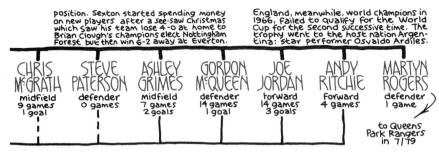

position. Sexton started spending money on new players after a see-saw Christmas which saw his team lose 4-0 at home to Brian Clough's champions elect Nottingham Forest but then win 6-2 away at Everton.

England, meanwhile, world champions in 1966, failed to qualify for the World Cup for the second successive time. The trophy went to the host nation Argentina: star performer Osvaldo Ardiles.

In January 78, six months into his first season as manager, Sexton began to reshape his team by signing Leeds United's rampaging Scottish striker Joe Jordan for £350,000. He became an instant favourite at Old Trafford, as did former Leeds and Scotland team-mate Gordon McQueen, who was signed by Sexton only a month later for a fee of £495,000. McQueen, in particular, found favour with the fans: on his arrival he claimed that, if asked, 99% of footballers would tell you that their ambition was to play for United...and the other 1% are lying. Docherty's last recruit, 20 year old Ashley Grimes also made his initial appearance as a red devil. Acquired at a cost of £20,000 from the Dublin Side Bohemians, he would be what journalists describe as a reliable club servant for six years. Local lad Andy Ritchie won 8 England Schoolboy caps and then made his United debut a month after his 17th birthday,

but despite his initial promise, was unable to hold down a regular first team gig. The same fate awaited Nottingham born Martyn Rogers, who played 9 times for England Schoolboys and also made his United debut at 17. It was to be his first and last game for the club - but better to have loved and lost than never to have loved at all. With the arrival of Joe Jordan, the writing was on the wall for Stuart Pearson, who soon left for West Ham, having done sterling service for both United (178 games and 66 goals) and England (15 caps). Also on the move were Alex Forsyth and Gordon Hill. The former, a Scottish international (10 caps), returned to Scotland - while the latter was signed to score goals for Derby County...by ex-manager Tommy Docherty - who would sign him for a third time when he took over the management of QPR. Despite being United's leading scorer for two seasons, Hill was seen as an individual rather than a team player...an offence which Sexton was not prepared to tolerate.

CHRIS McGRATH	STEVE PATERSON	ASHLEY GRIMES	GORDON McQUEEN	JOE JORDAN	ANDY RITCHIE	MARTYN ROGERS
midfield 9 games 1 goal	defender 0 games	midfield 7 games 2 goals	defender 14 games 1 goal	forward 14 games 3 goals	forward 4 games	defender 1 game → to Queens Park Rangers in 7/79

the last 15 league matches. Attendances at Old Trafford began dipping below 40,000 - and to finish 9th in the table was rather better than Sexton could have expected. Their drab form continued through most of a

particularly dispiriting Cup Final - their third in four years - against a ferocious Arsenal, inspired by Liam Brady. Five minutes from time, it seemed like game over for a flagging and beleaguered United, who trailed 2-0 ....

but quickfire goals by McQueen and McIlroy jolted the crowd into an edge of seat, orgasmic trance. With the referee about to blow time, however, Alan Sunderland restored the Arsenal

lead and the exhausted United collapsed in utter dejection. That the game entered history books for one of the most thrilling Cup Final climaxes ever was of only limited consolation...to the players and to Sexton.

CHRIS McGRATH	GARY BAILEY	ASHLEY GRIMES	GORDON McQUEEN	JOE JORDAN	ANDY RITCHIE	TOM SLOAN	MICKEY THOMAS	STEVE PATERSON	TOM CONNELL	DAVID McCREERY
midfield 2 games (both as sub)	goalkeeper 28 games	midfield 5 games	defender 36 games 6 goals	forward 30 games 6 goals	forward 16 games 10 goals	midfield 3 games	midfield 25 games 1 goal	defender 1 game	full back 2 games → to Glentoran in 6/82 for £37,000	midfield 14 games → to QPR in 8/79 for £200,000

The United of the late 70s was a team in transition. Despite being crammed with internationals - Brian Greenhoff, Stewart Houston, Paddy Roche, Lou Macari, Sammy McIlroy, Jimmy Nicholl, Steve Coppell, Martin Buchan, Arthur Albiston, Kevin Moran, Chris McGrath, Gary Bailey, Ashley Grimes, Gordon McQueen, Mickey Thomas, Joe Jordan, Tom Sloan and David McCreery, ie 18 of the 22 strong 78/79 complement, had been or would be selected to represent their country - they hardly compared with the teams of the late 50s or late 60s. No Player of the Year awards.... and only one trophy during the whole decade!

1978–79

Back Row (l/r)
Stewart Houston, Jimmy Nicholl, Brian Greenhoff, Andy Ritchie, Steve Paterson, Ashley Grimes, Gordon McQueen, Kevin Moran

Middle Row (l/r)
Tommy Cavanagh, Stuart Pearson, Tom Sloane, David McCreery, Paddy Roche, Gary Bailey, Chris McGrath, Mike Duxbury, Dave Sexton, Laurie Brown

Front Row (l/r)
Steve Coppell, Arthur Albiston, Sammy McIlroy, Martin Buchan, Lou Macari, Jimmy Greenhoff, Mickey Thomas, Joe Jordan

In January 1980, World In Action screened an exposé of United's 65 year old chairman Louis Edwards. A year in the making, the documentary alleged bribery, corruption and financial hanky-panky both at United and in his meat trading business. A month later, as official investigations got under way, Edwards suffered a fatal heart attack. The case was closed and never re-opened. Originally introduced to the club by Matt Busby, Edwards had been a director since 1958. Within seven years, he had become chairman and major share holder. On his death, his son Martin took over and has held the position ever since. Meanwhile, Sir Matt Busby was presented with a Professional Footballer's Association Merit Award in 1980, the year in which he was made President of Manchester United.

By now there were serious problems at Old Trafford. The playing was all too often lacklustre, the heart one degree under...but worst of all, the image had slipped. United were supposed to be the biggest and the best, the most resplendent and glamorous club in the land – bigger than Liverpool, Arsenal, Spurs, Chelsea or anyone else! The cerebral Sexton studied Wittgenstein and John Stuart Mill in his spare time – and quoted Robert Frost's poetry at press conferences. A man with his ego well under control, he was above spouting the usual hype and waffle. He was out of time: the trend was for showbizzy managers who could boost their clubs' reputations with ostentatious media interviews.

1979-80

Having spent the close season considering what modifications would enhance the team's performance, Sexton persuaded a Chelsea protégé to join him at Old Trafford. A precocious developer, Ray Wilkins had signed with Chelsea at 15 – but his apprenticeship was a short one: at 18 he was team captain... the youngest ever. In 76/77, he and Sexton had masterminded their promotion from the second division – and now his old manager was having

STEWART HOUSTON	PADDY ROCHE	SAMMY McILROY	JIMMY NICHOLL	STEVE COPPELL	MARTIN BUCHAN	LOU MACARI	ARTHUR ALBISTON	KEVIN MORAN
full back 14 games	goalkeeper 0 games	midfield 41 games 6 goals	defender 42 games	forward 42 games 8 goals	defender 42 games	midfield 39 games 9 goals	full back 25 games	defender 9 games 1 goal

to Sheffield United 7/80

Two players made their United debuts during the 80/81 season ...one had cost nothing, the other was by some way the most extravagant investment the club had ever made. The former, Mike Duxbury was born in Accrington in 1959 – three years before Accrington Stanley resigned from the league. Mike joined United from school, in May 75, and waited over five years for a first team place, over eight years for the first of 10 England caps. The latter, 24 year old England striker Garry Birtles was the goalscoring star of Nottingham Forest. Sensing that he would be the perfect upfront partner for Joe Jordan, Sexton laid out £1·25 million for him – but the move would have tragic consequences for both player and manager. Despite having netted over 50 goals for Forest, Garry Birtles finished his first season at United, with a blank score-sheet ...25 games, 0 goals. He was as bewildered and astonished as Sexton. A joke circulated on the United terraces, concerning the US hostages held in Iran. On their release, ran the gag, their first question would be " Has Garry Birtles scored a goal yet?" Fortunately, he scored one – in an FA Cup tie against Brighton!

1980-81

In their bleakest season since relegation in 1973, United suffered humiliating defeats in the early rounds of both the League Cup and the FA Cup. Back in the UEFA Cup for the first time in four years, they fell to a team that

Few United fans had even heard of, Widzew Lodz of Poland. Worse, they managed only 8 wins in the first 35 league games – at one stage unable to score a single goal in 5 consecutive matches, a new club record they would rather have avoided.

MIKE DUXBURY	GARRY BIRTLES	PADDY ROCHE	SAMMY McILROY	JIMMY NICHOLL	STEVE COPPELL	MARTIN BUCHAN	LOU MACARI	ARTHUR ALBISTON	KEVIN MORAN
full back 27 games 2 goals	forward 25 games	goalkeeper 2 games	midfield 31 games 5 goals	defender 36 games 1 goal	forward 42 games 6 goals	defender 26 games	midfield 37 games 9 goals	full back 42 games 1 goal	defender 32 games

1979–80

Back Row (l/r)
Kevin Moran, Nikola Jovanovic, Jimmy Nicholl, Andy Ritchie, Joe Jordan, Ashley Grimes

Middle Row (l/r)
Tommy Cavanagh, Dave Sexton, Stewart Houston, Jimmy Greenhoff, Paddy Roche, Gary Bailey, Gordon McQueen, Laurie Brown

Front Row (l/r)
Arthur Albiston, Steve Coppell, Ray Wilkins, Lou Macari, Martin Buchan, Mickey Thomas, Sammy McIlroy

to stump up £825,000 (a club record) to secure his services for United. It was widely thought that Wilkins would inspire an immediate, spellbinding renaissance...but it was a little slow in coming: United lost to Spurs in the third round of the FA Cup (Glenn Hoddle played in goal after their keeper was immobilised in a collision with Joe Jordan) but beat them in the third round of the League Cup - only to lose the next round to Norwich. Those distractions out of the way, they concentrated on the League championship. With Wilkins controlling the midfield, Coppell at his marauding best, Jordan finally into goalscoring stride (the only player to reach double figures) and a tight defence built around Bailey, McQueen and the perennial Buchan, United chased Liverpool at the top of the table. Never out of the top 2 after October, they were skewered on the last game of the season, finishing in second place - a very creditable position, their highest for 12 years.

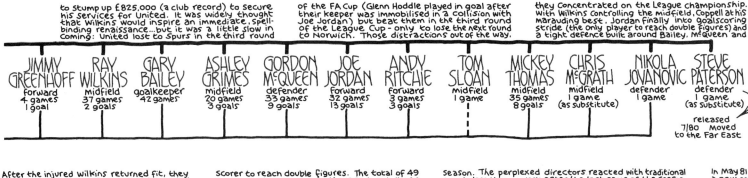

JIMMY GREENHOFF — forward — 4 games — 1 goal
RAY WILKINS — midfield — 37 games — 2 goals
GARY BAILEY — goalkeeper — 42 games
ASHLEY GRIMES — midfield — 20 games
GORDON McQUEEN — defender — 33 games — 9 goals
JOE JORDAN — forward — 32 games — 13 goals
ANDY RITCHIE — forward — 3 games — 3 goals
TOM SLOAN — midfield — 1 game
MICKEY THOMAS — midfield — 35 games — 8 goals
CHRIS McGRATH — midfield — 1 game (as substitute)
NIKOLA JOVANOVIC — defender — 1 game
STEVE PATERSON — defender — 1 game (as substitute) → released 7/80 Moved to the Far East

In January 80, Dave Sexton signed United's first continental star, the Yugoslavian international Nikola Jovanovic, who was prised from Red Star Belgrade in a £300,000 transfer deal. Chairman Martin Edwards maintains that lb (weight) for £ (sterling) it was the club's least successful purchase. In his first season, he made only one first team appearance; in his next, he made 19 - but Jovanovic was comfortable neither playing for United nor living in England. In 1981, he went home, taking his club car with him, and in 1982 it was confirmed that his contract had lapsed.

After the injured Wilkins returned fit, they won all 7 of the last 7 games, which pulled them up to 8th place in the league. For the fourth season running, Coppell played every game, and Jordan was again the only goal scorer to reach double figures. The total of 49 goals was less than half the 1959 total. It was not a pretty picture, particularly for the United supporters, whose pride was shaken: the average attendance dropped by 6500 over the previous season. The perplexed directors reacted with traditional speed: less than a week after the last game of the season, a tight-lipped Dave Sexton was given his marching orders. No more Mr Nice Guy. He went south to become manager of Coventry and was later on England's coaching staff.

In May 81, when Chairman Martin Edwards set about looking for a new manager, one of his priorities was to find a loquacious communicator, a man capable of making the club feel special again. Ron Atkinson may not have been his first choice (he was in fact the fourth choice: Lawrie McMenemy, Bobby Robson and Ron Saunders had all turned the job down) but he was certainly able to meet that prerequisite. He swanked into Old Trafford on the back of turning West Bromwich Albion into one of the most attractive teams in football - and he immediately set about invigorating United. 42 years old, the flamboyant Atkinson wore expensive clothes with the swagger of a hot shot Chicago gangster. He had paid his dues as a player and manager, working his way up from Southern League insignificance. Now he was big time and wanted everyone to know it; he was the kiddie to lead United out of the doldrums and back to glory. The players took to him; the directors liked the cut of his jib. They gave him carte blanche to do what it takes to make United great again. His first move was to hire his West Brom assistant Mick Brown to be his right hand man at United...and then he started buying!

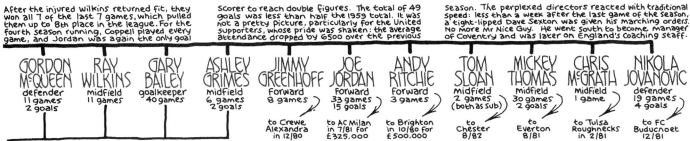

GORDON McQUEEN — defender — 11 games — 2 goals
RAY WILKINS — midfield — 11 games
GARY BAILEY — goalkeeper — 40 games
ASHLEY GRIMES — midfield — 6 games — 2 goals
JIMMY GREENHOFF — forward — 8 games → to Crewe Alexandra in 12/80
JOE JORDAN — forward — 33 games — 15 goals → to AC Milan in 7/81 for £325,000
ANDY RITCHIE — forward — 3 games → to Brighton in 10/80 for £500,000
TOM SLOAN — midfield — 2 games (both as sub) → to Chester 8/82
MICKEY THOMAS — midfield — 30 games — 2 goals → to Everton 8/81
CHRIS McGRATH — midfield — 1 game → to Tulsa Roughnecks in 2/81
NIKOLA JOVANOVIC — defender — 19 games — 4 goals → to FC Buducnoet 12/81

1980–81

Back Row (l/r)
Kevin Moran, Chris McGrath, Joe Jordan, Mike Duxbury, Andy Ritchie, Ashley Grimes, Nikola Jovanovic

Middle Row (l/r)
Dave Sexton, Tom Connell, Tom Sloan, Jimmy Nicholl, Paddy Roche, Gary Bailey, Gordon McQueen, Sammy McIlroy, Laurie Brown

Front Row (l/r)
Tommy Cavanagh, Arthur Albiston, Jimmy Greenhoff, Lou Macari, Martin Buchan, Mickey Thomas, Steve Coppell, Ray Wilkins

Having taken up his new position in June 81, the intrepid Ron Atkinson wasted no time wading into the transfer market; he intended to start the new season with guns blazing. His first foray was to negotiate an exchange in which Mickey Thomas went to Everton in return for full back John Gidman. Both players carried a £450,000 price tag. His next acquisition would cost twice that much. To replace Joe Jordan, who had skipped over to Milan on the expiry of his contract, Atkinson paid £900,000 for the great Arsenal and Republic of Ireland centre forward Frank Stapleton. An instant favourite at Old Trafford, he would be top goal scorer for the next three seasons. It was Atkinson's third deal, however, which the directors have most to thank him for

...the best United 'buy since Denis Law was tempted back from Italy 19 years earlier. Atkinson returned to his old club to bargain for the inspirational midfield player Bryan Robson. "It's a fantastic move for me," said Robson. "I am sure that it will be of benefit to everyone concerned". For the next twelve years, Robson never put a foot wrong for United; his only mistake was the curly perm he sported the day he signed. In a £2 million plus package deal – the biggest in British soccer history – Robson left West Brom along with Remi Moses, a Mancunian 20 year old born of Nigerian parents. Big Ron was assembling his dream team!

A trio of trophies would have been an agreeable start to Atkinson's tenure – but it was not to be. The re-shaped team took time to jell. They lost sight of both cups in the earliest rounds: to Watford in the FA Cup, to Spurs in the League

Cup. They did better in the Division, finishing a creditable third – and, more importantly, it was achieved by playing football that was both attractive and entertaining. Late in the season, a spirited youth appeared for

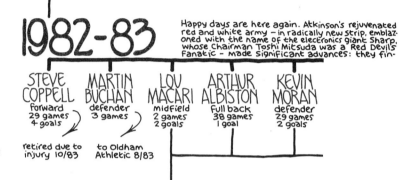

1981-82

GARRY BIRTLES	PADDY ROCHE	SAMMY McILROY	JIMMY NICHOLL	STEVE COPPELL	MARTIN BUCHAN	LOU MACARI	ARTHUR ALBISTON	KEVIN MORAN
forward 32 games 11 goals	goalkeeper 3 games	midfield 12 games 3 goals	defender 1 game (as substitute)	forward 35 games 9 goals	defender 27 games	midfield 10 games 2 goals	full back 42 games 1 goal	defender 30 games 7 goals
to Nottingham Forest in 9/82 for £250,000	to Brentford 8/82	to Stoke City 2/82 for £350,000	to Toronto Blizzard 4/82 for £250,000					

A heady year began with Ron Atkinson picking up the Dutch international ace Arnold Muhren on a free transfer after his four year contract at Ipswich ran out. Muhren's left foot – invariably described as cultured – added a touch of class. It was as well he arrived: United suffered a blight of injury. Gidman and Buchan managed only 3 games each, Wilkins was out for much of the season, Robson confirmed that he was almost as accident prone as he had been at West Brom, and, sadly, Steve Coppell was forced to retire at 28, after the knee damage he suffered playing for England in Nov 81 finally proved ineradicable. After assessing his options, he went south for a nine year stint as manager of Crystal Palace. One of the club's most consistent and dependable

forwards, Coppell had scored 70 goals in 392 games spread across eight years, and he had won 42 England caps. Also leaving Old Trafford was Martin Buchan, who moved to Oldham Athletic on a free transfer. In his 11 plus years, he made 455 appearances for United – but in Oct 84, at the age of 35, he too would retire from the game due to injury repercussions. Playing their last games too were Ashley Grimes and Scott McGarvey. The former had all but reconciled himself to the subs bench at United, and hoped for better things at Coventry City – but it was only when he moved to Luton a year later that his skills were fully utilised. Scott McGarvey, cut out of contention by the prodigious Whiteside, went to Wolves on loan before travelling on to Portsmouth –

the start of an odyssey which would take him to Carlisle, Grimsby, Bristol, Oldham, Wigan, Japan, Cyprus, Derry, Whitton and Barrow. Along with Muhren, new signings during the 1982/83 season were Paul McGrath, a 6'2" defensive pillar acquired from the Dublin club St Patrick's Athletic for £30,000, and a back-up goalie to replace Roche, Jeff Wealands, who came up from Birmingham City. Also making 3 cameo appearances for United was the once magical Laurie Cunningham, who had been worth just under a million pounds when he left West Brom for Real Madrid in 1979. Hamstrung by injury, he had been released by the Spanish club – but after a brief on-loan test-run, Ron Atkinson decided against signing him. He also decided against keeping a player he bought for £250,000 from the Vancouver Whitecaps. After just one League Cup game, he sold him back: Peter Beardsley!

Happy days are here again. Atkinson's rejuvenated red and white army – in radically new strip, emblazoned with the name of the electronics giant Sharp, whose Chairman Toshi Mitsuda was a Red Devils' fanatic – made significant advances: they fin-

1982-83

STEVE COPPELL	MARTIN BUCHAN	LOU MACARI	ARTHUR ALBISTON	KEVIN MORAN
forward 29 games 4 goals	defender 3 games	midfield 2 games 2 goals	full back 38 games 1 goal	defender 29 games 2 goals
retired due to injury 10/83	to Oldham Athletic 8/83			

1981–82

Back Row (l/r)
Nikola Jovanovic, Gary Bailey, Paddy Roche, Gordon McQueen

Middle Row (l/r)
Mike Duxbury, Jimmy Nicholl, Garry Birtles, Scott McGarvey, Frank Stapleton, Kevin Moran, Sammy McIlroy, Mick Brown

Front Row (l/r)
John Gidman, Ray Wilkins, Lou Macari, Ron Atkinson, Martin Buchan, Steve Coppell, Arthur Albiston

the First time. A formidable talent, even as a Belfast schoolboy, Norman Whiteside joined as an apprentice - but was hustling for a regular First team place even before he signed professional papers. He was only 16 when he came

on as a substitute in an away game against Brighton, and a week past his 17th birthday when he made his full debut, against Stoke City at Old Trafford in the last game of the year. Ominously for the rest of the league,

he scored one of the winning goals. That summer, he was the youngest player ever to represent his country in the World Cup finals – playing for Northern Ireland against Morocco, aged 17 years and 41 days. Along with Whiteside were two other new boys, Scott McGarvey and Alan Dav-

ies. The former was a product of Celtic Boys Club in Glasgow, the latter a local schoolboy. Such was the competition at United that neither was able to commandeer a regular place in the side, even though both exhibited admirable flair and skill.

The saddest story of the season concerned Garry Birtles. Sexton's great white hope had located his lost firepower and banged in 11 goals – but despite his return to form, Atkinson put him on the auction block. Still only 26 years old, he was picked up by his old club Nottingham Forest for £250,000, his market value having dropped by a million in just two years. Also leaving Old Trafford were 3 old campaigners: Sammy McIlroy was going after 11½ years (390 appearances and 70 goals) with the club, Jimmy Nicholl after 10 years (234 matches and 6 goals), and Paddy Roche after nine years.

GORDON McQUEEN	RAY WILKINS	GARY BAILEY	ASHLEY GRIMES	MIKE DUXBURY	BRYAN ROBSON	NORMAN WHITESIDE	FRANK STAPLETON	JOHN GIDMAN	REMI MOSES	ALAN DAVIES	SCOTT McGARVEY
defender 21 games	midfield 42 games 1 goal	goalkeeper 39 games	midfield 9 games 1 goal	full back 19 games	midfield 32 games 5 goals	forward 1 game	forward 41 games 13 goals	full back 36 games 1 goal	midfield 20 games 2 goals	midfield 1 game	forward 10 games 2 goals

ished 3rd in the league, were runners-up in the League (by now Milk) Cup, and - by some happy coincidence on Sir Matt Busby's 74th birthday - they won the FA Cup. It was United's first trophy since 1977, and they were cock-a-hoop.

In the FA Cup run, not one goal was conceded until the semi-final, when Arsenal were brushed aside. In the final, United were pitched against Brighton, a club doomed to relegation and with their inspirational captain Steve Foster suspended.

But the underdogs were not easily beaten. Despite a Wilkins wonder goal and a fine performance from young Alan Davies on the wing, United only survived a 2-2 draw thanks to Bailey's incredible last minute save. In the replay, the hapless Brighton

were demolished. Robson, magnificent, scored twice; Muhren popped in a penalty; and Whiteside made it 4-0. The youngest player to score in a Cup Final, he deserved a drink ... and was now just old enough to buy one!

GORDON McQUEEN	RAY WILKINS	GARY BAILEY	PAUL McGRATH	MIKE DUXBURY	BRYAN ROBSON	NORMAN WHITESIDE	FRANK STAPLETON	JOHN GIDMAN	REMI MOSES	ALAN DAVIES	ARNOLD MUHREN	JEFF WEALANDS	ASHLEY GRIMES	SCOTT McGARVEY	LAURIE CUNNINGHAM
defender 37 games	midfield 26 games 1 goal	goalkeeper 37 games	defender 14 games 3 goals	full back 42 games 1 goal	midfield 33 games 10 goals	forward 39 games 8 goals	forward 41 games 14 goals	full back 3 games	midfield 29 games	midfield 2 games	midfield 32 games 5 goals	goalkeeper 5 games	midfield 15 games 2 goals to Coventry City in 8/83 for £200,000	forward 3 games 1 goal to Portsmouth in 7/84 for £85,000	forward 3 games 1 goal to Sporting Gijon 8/83

1982–83

Back Row (l/r)
Kevin Moran, Scott McGarvey, Gordon McQueen, Gary Bailey, Steve Pears, Paul McGrath, Ashley Grimes, Garry Birtles

Middle Row (l/r)
Jim McGregor, Norman Whiteside, Alan Davies, Mike Duxbury, Peter Bodak, Steve Coppell, Lou Macari, Mick Brown

Front Row (l/r)
Remi Moses, Arnold Muhren, John Gidman, Ray Wilkins, Ron Atkinson, Martin Buchan, Arthur Albiston, Bryan Robson, Frank Stapleton

INSET
Left: Jeff Wealands *Right:* Laurie Cunningham

Moneywise, 1983/84 was an economical season for Atkinson. Three youngsters who'd been on United's books since leaving school all got First Division outings. Aberdonian Graeme Hogg, who played in the reserves as understudy to Gordon McQueen, came to the fore after the latter was injured in the first game of 1984 - and Clayton Blackmore from Neath, who had committed to United as a 14 year old schoolboy, was given his chance in the last match of the season. In November, 20 year old Mark Hughes, who had also been climbing the United ladder since he was 14, gave some indication of what was to come: on his debut, a League Cup game at Oxford, he scored the first of 150 goals for the club. Once his potential had been recognised, there was no holding him back. A few weeks later, he won his first cap for Wales, scoring the goal that gave them victory over England...in a match played in his home town of Wrexham. Hughes joined another dashing frontrunner Arthur Graham, who had transferred from Leeds during the close season. A Scottish international, he cost Atkinson £45,000 and though at 30 his top flight days were numbered, he proved a most sagacious short-term investment -

covering territory formerly held by Steve Coppell. The fifth and final newcomer this season was 25 year old Spurs star Garth Crooks. On loan for 6 weeks, he scored two goals in six games before Spurs wanted him back. Sadly, after an outstanding season in which he played every league game, Ray Wilkins made a summer move to AC Milan. That the club netted a £1·5 million transfer fee was of little consolation to his fans at Old Trafford - but English clubs were hardly in a position to compete with their Continental counterparts and Wilkins' departure was a brain-drain precedent which would have significant consequences for United. After 373 appearances and 97 goals, Lou Macari left to become player/manager of the Fourth Division side Swindon Town, where he would become a far more newsworthy and controversial figure than he had ever been at United. Though an excellent stop-gap, Arthur Graham made no further appearances after this season - nor did Alan Davies, an exciting international (13 Welsh caps) whose United career never hit overdrive. In June 84, a feeling of security and well-being swept through Old Trafford when Bobby Charlton joined the board.

A terrible season for football generally culminated in Maggie Thatcher sticking her nose in. In April 85, she chaired a cabinet meeting to try to eliminate hooliganism in football. Football League clubs officially rejected her plan for a national membership card scheme for supporters. In the past few months, we had seen Millwall fans destroying half of Luton, unprecedented violence at a Birmingham v Leeds Utd match, rioting at Chelsea, police arrests everywhere, a tragic fire at Bradford, and 38 fans crushed to death during tribal wars at Heysel Stadium. UEFA banned any English club from competing in Europe, and FIFA banned English clubs from playing anywhere outside England. National prestige had never been so dishonoured.

At United, however, it was not all doom and gloom. Mark Hughes burst through as the latest red devil, backstreet soccer genius, cutting his way through the opposition like a wolf through sheep, to score 16 goals and find himself voted The PFA's Young Player of the Year. The second leading scorer was new boy Gordon Strachan with 15 goals. During the close season, Atkinson had spent the money from Wilkins's sale wisely: he'd paid £600,000 for Strachan, a wiry fiery Scot who had banged in 89 goals for Aberdeen, and another £800,000 for Jesper Olsen, the Ajax winger, who - playing for Denmark - had single-handedly destroyed England in a European Championship qualifier the previous year. Proving we all make mistakes, Big Ron also paid Spurs £700,000 for Alan Brazil, who failed to find his feet at Old Trafford, and he allowed Crewe to buy a kid who was running amok in the youth team...David Platt. A gift at only £50,000.

Two other players also made their United first team debuts during the 84/85 season: Billy Garton and Steve Pears. The former was a Salford lad who had played in the youth team alongside Norman Whiteside and Mark Hughes, the latter a Durham boy who became a teenage United apprentice after trying out for Middlesbrough. He'd been with the club for over 8 years before he got his chance (after Gary Bailey broke a finger), but after only a handful of games, he moved on...to Middlesbrough. Also on the move, after 228 appearances and 26 goals, was the reliable Gordon McQueen, whose last two seasons had been frustrated by injury, and Arnold Muhren, now approaching 34 and also injury prone, went home to Holland to sign with his first club, Ajax. After 4 years of comings and goings, however, Atkinson had the most charismatic team in the land: all 12 of his magnificent 1985 Cup Final squad had represented their country at full international level!

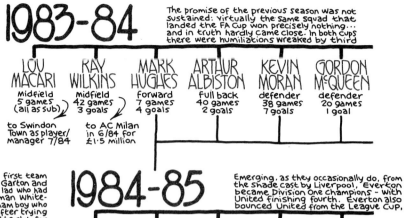

1983-84

The promise of the previous season was not sustained: virtually the same squad that landed the FA Cup won precisely nothing... and in truth hardly came close. In both cups there were humiliations wreaked by third

LOU MACARI	RAY WILKINS	MARK HUGHES	ARTHUR ALBISTON	KEVIN MORAN	GORDON McQUEEN
midfield 5 games (all as sub)	midfield 42 games 3 goals	forward 7 games 4 goals	full back 40 games 2 goals	defender 38 games 7 goals	defender 20 games 1 goal
to Swindon Town as player/ manager 7/84	to AC Milan in 6/84 for £1·5 million				

1984-85

Emerging, as they occasionally do, from the shade cast by Liverpool, Everton became Division One champions - with United finishing fourth. Everton also bounced United from the League Cup.

JESPER OLSEN	MARK HUGHES	ARTHUR ALBISTON	KEVIN MORAN	GORDON STRACHAN
forward 36 games 5 goals	forward 38 games 16 goals	full back 39 games	defender 19 games 4 goals	midfield 41 games 15 goals

1983–84

Back Row (l/r)
Mike Duxbury, Mark Hughes, Paul McGrath, Gordon McQueen, Graeme Hogg, Norman Whiteside, John Gidman

Middle Row (l/r)
Mick Brown, Kevin Moran, Arnold Muhren, Jeff Wealands, Steve Pears, Gary Bailey, Alan Brazil, Frank Stapleton, Jim McGregor

Front Row (l/r)
Arthur Albiston, Jesper Olsen, Bryan Robson, Ron Atkinson, Remi Moses, Arthur Graham, Gordon Strachan

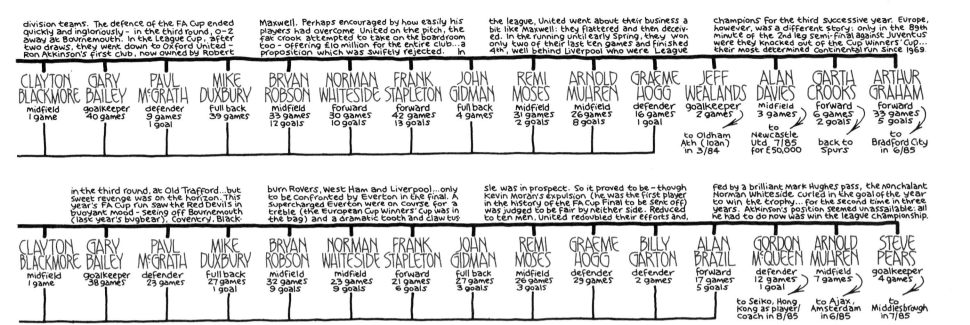

division teams. The defence of the FA Cup ended quickly and ingloriously - in the third round, 0-2 away at Bournemouth. In the League Cup, after two draws, they went down to Oxford United - Ron Atkinson's first club, now owned by Robert Maxwell. Perhaps encouraged by how easily his players had overcome United on the pitch, the fat crook attempted to take on the boardroom too - offering £10 million for the entire club...a proposition which was swiftly rejected. In the league, United went about their business a bit like Maxwell: they flattered and then deceived. In the running until early Spring, they won only two of their last ten games and finished 4th, well behind Liverpool who were League champions for the third successive year. Europe, however, was a different story: only in the 89th minute of the 2nd leg semi-final against Juventus were they knocked out of the Cup Winners' Cup... their most determined Continental run since 1969.

CLAYTON BLACKMORE	GARY BAILEY	PAUL McGRATH	MIKE DUXBURY	BRYAN ROBSON	NORMAN WHITESIDE	FRANK STAPLETON	JOHN GIDMAN	REMI MOSES	ARNOLD MUHREN	GRAEME HOGG	JEFF WEALANDS	ALAN DAVIES	GARTH CROOKS	ARTHUR GRAHAM
midfield 1 game	goalkeeper 40 games	defender 9 games 1 goal	full back 39 games	midfield 33 games 12 goals	forward 30 games 10 goals	forward 42 games 13 goals	full back 4 games	midfield 31 games 2 goals	midfield 26 games 8 goals	defender 16 games 1 goal	goalkeeper 2 games → to Oldham Ath (loan) in 3/84	midfield 3 games → to Newcastle Utd 7/85 for £50,000	forward 6 games 2 goals → back to Spurs	forward 33 games 5 goals → to Bradford City in 6/85

in the third round, at Old Trafford...but sweet revenge was on the horizon. This year's FA Cup run saw the Red Devils in buoyant mood - seeing off Bournemouth (last year's bugbear), Coventry, Blackburn Rovers, West Ham and Liverpool...only to be confronted by Everton in the final. A supercharged Everton were on course for a treble (the European Cup Winners' Cup was in the bag) and a dramatic tooth and claw tussle was in prospect. So it proved to be - though Kevin Moran's expulsion (he was the first player in the history of the FA Cup Final to be sent off) was judged to be fair by neither side. Reduced to ten men, United redoubled their efforts and, fed by a brilliant Mark Hughes pass, the nonchalant Norman Whiteside curled in the goal of the year to win the trophy... for the second time in three years. Atkinson's position seemed unassailable: all he had to do now was win the league championship.

CLAYTON BLACKMORE	GARY BAILEY	PAUL McGRATH	MIKE DUXBURY	BRYAN ROBSON	NORMAN WHITESIDE	FRANK STAPLETON	JOHN GIDMAN	REMI MOSES	GRAEME HOGG	BILLY GARTON	ALAN BRAZIL	GORDON McQUEEN	ARNOLD MUHREN	STEVE PEARS
midfield 1 game	goalkeeper 38 games	defender 23 games	full back 27 games 1 goal	midfield 32 games 9 goals	midfield 23 games 9 goals	forward 21 games 6 goals	full back 27 games 3 goals	midfield 26 games 3 goals	defender 29 games	defender 2 games	forward 17 games 5 goals	defender 12 games 1 goal → to Seiko, Hong Kong as player/ coach in 8/85	midfield 7 games → to Ajax, Amsterdam in 6/85	goalkeeper 4 games → to Middlesbrough in 7/85

1984–85

Manchester United's Mark Hughes blasts past Sheffield Wednesday's Des Walker

What do you do when you're on a roll? Get rid of your leading goalscorer, the hottest local hero the club has had for years! After scoring almost at will during the Autumn, the superb Mark Hughes was sold, early in the New Year, to Terry Venables - then the manager of Barcelona - for a fee of £2·5 million. The deal was to be kept secret until the end of the season - but Hughes, not that keen to go in the first place, couldn't take the pressure of the subterfuge. His form dipped. When the news leaked out, the fans were stunned. How was it that the club could throw away any chance of the championship by flogging their star player? This seeming lack of ambition and perspective percolated down from the board room to the dressing room. Worse, Ron Atkinson set out to rebuild his team using the money from the Hughes deal like a lottery winner let loose in a jumble sale. He bought often and he bought bad, cluttering Old Trafford with a selection of bargain-bin items no-one else wanted. During the season, 8 players wore the United shirt for the first time - but none were long term prospects. John Sivebaek (£285,000), Peter Barnes (£50,000), Mark Higgins (£60,000), and Terry Gibson (rated at £600,000 in an exchange deal with Alan Brazil) came and went quickly - as did local school boy Mark Dempsey. Peter Davenport, Colin Gibson and Chris Turner hung on a little longer. Heavy vibes at United!

1985-86

Ten victories in the first ten games; two draws and three wins in the next five...an inspirational start! By Bonfire Night the speculation was not whether United would win their first league title for 19 years, but when it would all be over. The answer was: by Christmas. In a New Year collapse so profound that it must have touched five on the Richter Scale, only 7 of the remaining 20 games were won. For the third year running, the club had to be satisfied with 4th place in the usual

| **MARK HUGHES** forward 40 games 17 goals | **TERRY GIBSON** forward 2 games | **JOHNNY SIVEBAEK** full back 2 games | **PETER BARNES** forward 12 games 2 goals | **PETER DAVENPORT** forward 11 games 1 goal | **JESPER OLSEN** forward 25 games 11 goals | **COLIN GIBSON** defender 18 games 5 goals | **ARTHUR ALBISTON** full back 37 games 1 goal | **KEVIN MORAN** defender 18 games | **GORDON STRACHAN** midfield 27 games 5 goals |

to Barcelona (see 1988/89)

King of the castle throughout 1985, Big Ron saw his cachet melt like ice cream during 1986. He spent the Summer doing television commentary on Maradona's hand of God performance in the World Cup finals in Mexico and wondering if it would be a prudent move to tender his resignation at Old Trafford. He decided to stay....but a lamentable league run was followed by a 1-4 thrashing at Southampton, in the League (or rather, after 5 years as the Milk Cup, the Littlewoods) Cup, and it was obvious to all and sundry that his head was going to roll. On Guy Fawkes night 85, he'd been top of the world... but this year he was the guy, burnt at the stake for allowing the club's reputation to become so tarnished. He'd lasted almost 5½ years, during which time he had seen them win 2 Cup Finals. Not good enough. Questions had been raised about team discipline, punch-ups during training sessions, the decline of the youth team and the scouting network, and the rationale behind recent signings. It was felt by the directors that a new man was needed to examine the entire sorry mess and restore United's esteem and self-respect. Within 24 hours, the Aberdeen manager Alex Ferguson had accepted the job. Under his guidance, Aberdeen were three times Scottish League champions and winners of the European Cup Winners Cup. In an expensive bit of business for United chairman Martin Edwards, Atkinson got £115,000 compensation, his right hand man Mick Brown got £40,000 and Aberdeen got £60,000 to soften the loss.

1986-87

When Alex Ferguson took over in early November 86, United were second from bottom of the table...and there was no money left in the kitty to buy them out of trouble. He set about his task with a characteristic whirl of energy. The man who, in earlier managerial days at St Mirren, had strapped a loudspeaker to the roof of his car and driven round Paisley trying to drum up support for his team, addressed every

| **TERRY GIBSON** forward 12 games 1 goal | **JOHNNY SIVEBAEK** full back 27 games 1 goal | **PETER BARNES** forward 7 games | **PETER DAVENPORT** forward 34 games 14 goals | **JESPER OLSEN** forward 22 games 3 goals | **COLIN GIBSON** defender 24 games 1 goal | **ARTHUR ALBISTON** full back 19 games | **KEVIN MORAN** defender 32 games | **GORDON STRACHAN** midfield 33 games 4 goals |

to Wimbledon in 8/87 for £200,000 — to St Etienne 8/87 for £227,000 — to Manchester City in 1/87 for £30,000

1985–86

Back Row (l/r)
Mike Duxbury, Remi Moses, Gordon Strachan, Jesper Olsen, Arthur Albiston, Clayton Blackmore

Middle Row (l/r)
Mick Brown, John Gidman, Bryan Robson, Ron Atkinson, Kevin Moran, Frank Stapleton, Jim McGregor

Front Row (l/r)
Graeme Hogg, Gary Bailey, Peter Barnes, Mark Hughes, Norman Whiteside, Alan Brazil, Chris Turner, Paul McGrath

two horse race - won this time by Liverpool, with Everton as runners-up. There were to be no consolations in the Cup competitions either: bundled out of the League Cup by Liverpool and out of the FA Cup by West Ham. There were plenty of excuses offered up for the precipitous decline. The favourite was that Manchester's hospitals were once again littered with United players: Robson out for most of the year with a dislocated shoulder, which was to pop out again during the summer's World Cup; Moses was laid low again with ankle ailments; and Bailey's career was wrecked by a knee injury just as he was reaching a peak. There were also the tales of internal indiscipline: the United drinking team were well known in local licensed premises. But there was more to it than that...the news of Mark Hughes' imminent departure rattled every United player and supporter to the very core.

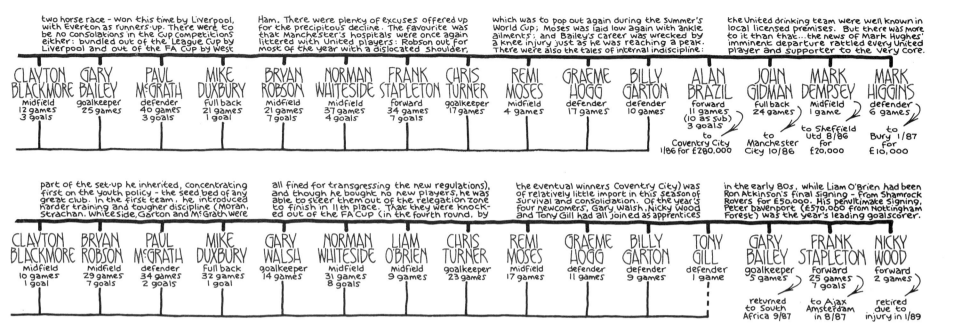

CLAYTON BLACKMORE	GARY BAILEY	PAUL McGRATH	MIKE DUXBURY	BRYAN ROBSON	NORMAN WHITESIDE	FRANK STAPLETON	CHRIS TURNER	REMI MOSES	GRAEME HOGG	BILLY GARTON	ALAN BRAZIL	JOHN GIDMAN	MARK DEMPSEY	MARK HIGGINS
midfield 12 games 3 goals	goalkeeper 25 games	defender 40 games 3 goals	full back 21 games 1 goal	midfield 21 games 7 goals	midfield 37 games 4 goals	forward 34 games 7 goals	goalkeeper 17 games	midfield 4 games	defender 17 games	defender 10 games	forward 11 games (10 as sub) 3 goals → to Coventry City 1/86 for £280,000	full back 24 games → to Manchester City 10/86	midfield 1 game → to Sheffield Utd 8/86 for £20,000	defender 6 games → to Bury 1/87 for £10,000

part of the set-up he inherited, concentrating first on the youth policy - the seed bed of any great club. In the first team, he introduced harder training and tougher discipline (Moran, Strachan, Whiteside, Garton and McGrath were all fined for transgressing the new regulations), and though he bought no new players, he was able to steer them out of the relegation zone to finish in 11th place. That they were knocked out of the FA Cup (in the fourth round, by the eventual winners Coventry City) was of relatively little import in this season of survival and consolidation. Of the year's four newcomers, Gary Walsh, Nicky Wood and Tony Gill had all joined as apprentices in the early 80s, while Liam O'Brien had been Ron Atkinson's final signing - from Shamrock Rovers for £50,000. His penultimate signing, Peter Davenport (£570,000 from Nottingham Forest) was the year's leading goalscorer.

CLAYTON BLACKMORE	BRYAN ROBSON	PAUL McGRATH	MIKE DUXBURY	GARY WALSH	NORMAN WHITESIDE	LIAM O'BRIEN	CHRIS TURNER	REMI MOSES	GRAEME HOGG	BILLY GARTON	TONY GILL	GARY BAILEY	FRANK STAPLETON	NICKY WOOD
midfield 10 games 1 goal	midfield 29 games 7 goals	defender 34 games 2 goals	full back 32 games 1 goal	goalkeeper 14 games	midfield 31 games 8 goals	midfield 9 games	goalkeeper 23 games	midfield 17 games	defender 11 games	defender 9 games	defender 1 game	goalkeeper 5 games → returned to South Africa 9/87	forward 25 games 7 goals → to Ajax Amsterdam in 8/87	forward 2 games → retired due to injury in 1/89

1986–87

Back Row (l/r)
Peter Davenport, John Sivebaek, Gary Walsh, Paul McGrath, Liam O'Brien, Kevin Moran

Front Row (l/r)
Mike Duxbury, Brian McClair, Bryan Robson, Gordon Strachan, Colin Gibson

Having won the confidence of the directors, Ferguson convinced them to rustle up two million pounds to buy Viv Anderson, Brian McClair and Steve Bruce. A Nottingham lad, Anderson (who cost £250,000) built his reputation with Forest, Arsenal and England and was a fortnight away from his 31st birthday when he debuted for United. Though a Geordie, Bruce (£825,000) moved south to gain experience and value at Gillingham and Norwich. He would become a bastion of United's defence - as well as cracking in the odd goal. A star at Celtic, for whom he scored 99 goals, McClair (£850,000) came to United as Scotland's reigning Player Of The Year - and he was soon to be netting 24 goals in his first season - the highest number since George Best twenty years

earlier. All three players would prove to be invaluable in United's resurgence. At the end of the season, fans bade a sad farewell to Remi Moses, reluctantly retiring at 27 rather than risk damaging his pinned and braced ankle further; Kevin Moran, the great Republic of Ireland international who was moving to Spain on a free transfer; and Arthur Albiston who, after 16 years and 464 appearances (the sixth highest number in United's history), was linking up with Ron Atkinson at West Brom. Also on the move was Chris Turner, a goalkeeper who had spent only 3 seasons with United after Atkinson paid Sunderland £275,000 for him. He rejoined his first club, Sheffield Wednesday, when he realised his career could go nowhere at Old Trafford once Ferguson went hunting for a new goalie.

In the League Cup, easy wins over lower division clubs Hull, Crystal Palace and Bury were followed by a surprise 0-2 defeat at Oxford Utd in the fifth round. In the FA Cup, the disposal of Ipswich Town seemed quite effortless but then came Arsenal at Highbury where McClair scored one goal but missed a penalty. A forgivable aberration..... but United were dumped.

1987-88

In Ferguson's first full season, United repaid his efforts by finishing second in the table - their best performance for eight years. In truth, they may have been runners-up... but they never looked like champions. Despite

VIV ANDERSON	PETER DAVENPORT	JESPER OLSEN	COLIN GIBSON	STEVE BRUCE	BRIAN McCLAIR
Full back	Forward	Forward	defender	defender	Forward
30 games	21 games	30 games	26 games	21 games	40 games
2 goals	5 goals	2 goals	2 goals	2 goals	24 goals

As Alex Ferguson got his legs under the table at Old Trafford, United underwent the most comprehensive personnel shuffle in its history: 9 new faces; 9 exits. For the fans, the most exciting signing was Mark Hughes - back in his spiritual home after 2 years in the wilderness of Barcelona and Bayern Munich. The move cost Ferguson £1·8 million - one of three big pre-season cheques. Another, for £450,000, went to his old club Aberdeen, for their 30 year old goalkeeper Jim Leighton, who had collected every medal on offer during a decade with the Dons. The third cheque bought full back-cum-winger Lee Sharpe, a 17 year old Brum lad, who moved up from Torquay when

£185,000 changed hands. In October, £650,000 was laid out for the steady Luton defender Mal Donaghy and the following month £175,000 secured the Bristol City forward Ralph Milne - but his first team tenure lasted only one season. In December, 19 year old Jules Maiorana joined from Histon FC (the East Anglian side) for a modest fee of £30,000. Three more players, all of whom had joined United straight from school, worked their way up to the first eleven: Russell Beardsmore, Lee Martin and Mark Robins. Through the out door went a parcel of Old Trafford favourites... McGrath, Olsen, Strachan and Whiteside. Like pop stars, footballers come and go - and the terrace heroes always play with both ends burning!

1988-89

Oh dear, oh dear, oh dear! A disastrous season! Ousted from the League Cup early, in a grim encounter at Wimbledon, United were lucky to finish 11th in a League won - in dramatic fashion - with the last kick of the season, live on tele.

vision, by Arsenal at Anfield. All had started so promisingly, with the return of the golden boy Mark Hughes - an uplifting moment for every United supporter. He and McClair played in every game together but the two-pronged

MARK HUGHES	LEE SHARPE	MARK ROBINS	VIV ANDERSON	JIM LEIGHTON	LEE MARTIN	COLIN GIBSON	STEVE BRUCE	BRIAN McCLAIR
Forward	Forward	Forward	Full back	goalkeeper	defender	defender	defender	Forward
38 games	19 games	1 game	5 games	38 games	20 games	1 game	38 games	38 games
14 goals		(9 more as sub)			1 goal		2 goals	10 goals

1987–88

Back Row (l/r)
Norman Whiteside, Chris Turner, Paul McGrath, Viv Anderson, Billy Garton, Graeme Hogg, Liam O'Brien, Gary Walsh, John Sivebaek

Middle Row (l/r)
Nicky Wood, Brian Whitehouse, Jim McGregor, Joe Brown, Archie Knox, Eric Harrison, Norman Davies, Jimmy Curran, Terry Gibson

Front Row (l/r)
Gordon Strachan, Peter Davenport, Mike Duxbury, Brian McClair, Kevin Moran, Alex Ferguson, Bryan Robson, Remi Moses, Colin Gibson, Arthur Albiston, Jesper Olsen

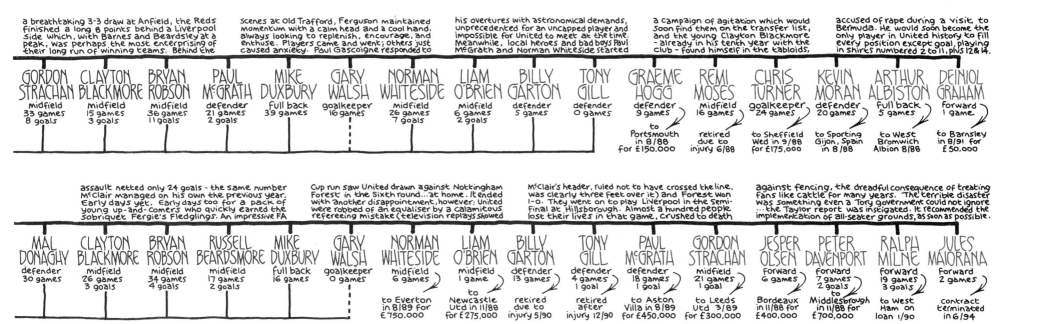

a breathtaking 3-3 draw at Anfield, the Reds finished a long 8 points behind a Liverpool side which, with Barnes and Beardsley at a peak, was perhaps the most enterprising of their long run of winning teams. Behind the

Scenes at Old Trafford, Ferguson maintained momentum with a calm head and a cool hand. always looking to replenish, encourage, and enthuse. Players came and went; others just caused anxiety. Paul Gascoigne responded to

his overtures with astronomical demands, unprecedented for an uncapped player and impossible for United to meet at the time. Meanwhile, local heroes and bad boys Paul McGrath and Norman Whiteside started

a campaign of agitation which would soon find them on the transfer list, and the young Clayton Blackmore - already in his tenth year with the club - found himself in the tabloids,

accused of rape during a visit to Bermuda. He would soon become the only player in United history to fill every position except goal, playing in shirts numbered 2 to 11, plus 12 & 14.

GORDON STRACHAN	CLAYTON BLACKMORE	BRYAN ROBSON	PAUL McGRATH	MIKE DUXBURY	GARY WALSH	NORMAN WHITESIDE	LIAM O'BRIEN	BILLY GARTON	TONY GILL	GRAEME HOGG	REMI MOSES	CHRIS TURNER	KEVIN MORAN	ARTHUR ALBISTON	DEINIOL GRAHAM
midfield 33 games 8 goals	midfield 15 games 3 goals	midfield 36 games 11 goals	defender 21 games 2 goals	full back 39 games	goalkeeper 16 games	midfield 26 games 7 goals	midfield 6 games 2 goals	defender 5 games	defender 0 games	defender 9 games	midfield 16 games	goalkeeper 24 games	defender 20 games	full back 5 games	forward 1 game
										to Portsmouth in 8/88 for £150,000	retired due to injury 6/88	to Sheffield Wed in 9/88 for £175,000	to Sporting Gijon, Spain in 8/88	to West Bromwich Albion 8/88	to Barnsley in 8/91 for £50,000

assault netted only 24 goals - the same number McClair managed on his own the previous year. Early days yet. Early days too for a pack of young up-and-comers who quickly earned the sobriquet Fergie's Fledglings. An impressive FA

Cup run saw United drawn against Nottingham Forest in the Sixth round...at home. It ended with another disappointment, however: United were robbed of an equaliser by a calamitous refereeing mistake (television replays showed

McClair's header, ruled not to have crossed the line, was clearly three feet over it) and Forest won 1-0. They went on to play Liverpool in the Semi-final at Hillsborough. Almost a hundred people lost their lives in that game, crushed to death

against fencing, the dreadful consequence of treating fans like cattle for many years. The terrible disaster was something even a Tory government could not ignore ...the Taylor report was instigated. It recommended the implementation of all-seater grounds, as soon as possible.

MAL DONAGHY	CLAYTON BLACKMORE	BRYAN ROBSON	RUSSELL BEARDSMORE	MIKE DUXBURY	GARY WALSH	NORMAN WHITESIDE	LIAM O'BRIEN	BILLY GARTON	TONY GILL	PAUL McGRATH	GORDON STRACHAN	JESPER OLSEN	PETER DAVENPORT	RALPH MILNE	JULES MAIORANA
defender 30 games	midfield 26 games 3 goals	midfield 34 games 4 goals	midfield 17 games 2 goals	full back 16 games	goalkeeper 0 games	midfield 6 games	midfield 1 game 1 goal	defender 13 games	defender 4 games 1 goal	defender 18 games 1 goal	midfield 21 games 2 goals	forward 6 games	forward 7 games 3 goals	forward 19 games 3 goals	forward 2 games
						to Everton in 8/89 for £750,000	to Newcastle Utd in 11/88 for £275,000	retired due to injury 5/90	retired after injury 12/90	to Aston Villa in 8/89 for £450,000	to Leeds Utd 3/89 for £300,000	Bordeaux in 11/88 for £400,000	to Middlesbrough in 11/88 for £700,000	to West Ham on loan 1/90	contract terminated in 6/94

1988–89

Back Row (l/r)
Viv Anderson, Neil Webb, Mike Duxbury, Billy Garton, Lee Sharpe, Mike Phelan, Lee Martin, Mal Donaghy, Steve Bruce

Middle Row (l/r)
Jim McGregor, Archie Knox, Guiliana Maiorana, Gary Walsh, Jim Leighton, David Wilson, Russell Beardsmore, Norman Davies

Front Row (l/r)
Mark Robins, Tony Gill, Colin Gibson, Bryan Robson, Alex Ferguson, Brian McClair, Mark Hughes, Clayton Blackmore, Ralph Milne

1989 marked the start of the fanzine era, and United's first two - Red News and Red Issue - started circulating the views from the terraces. Jim Leighton would not have found them comforting reading. A rather uneasy transition to English football ended abruptly when he was dropped after a rather unhappy Cup Final: though a regular Scottish cap, he never recaptured his first team place again. Nor did Colin Gibson after his smooth progress was hindered by persistent knee problems. A long service medal went to Mike Duxbury, leaving after 343 games and 15 years. During the close season, Ferguson had not just dipped into the purse...he had all but cleaned it out. Neil Webb arrived from Nottingham Forest for £1.5 million; Mike Phelan from Norwich for £750,000; Gary Pallister from Middlesbrough for £2.3 million; Danny Wallace from Southampton for £1.3 million; and Paul Ince from West Ham for £2.4 million. Some shopping list! Five new players for only 8¼ million quid!

1989-90

Astonishing though it may seem given subsequent events, the Old Trafford winter was dominated by a campaign to remove Fergie. Orchestrated by the fanzines and seized on by the press, it suggested that Ferguson would soon join the list of managers sacked after failing to live up to Matt Busby. Things went from bad (a sequence of 7 league games with only one win) to worse (a 1-5 hammering at Manchester City), to excruciating (a 0-3 home defeat against Spurs in the third round of the League Cup) - and it was still only October. Crowds at Old Trafford, already falling, would drop as low as 29,281. By January, with

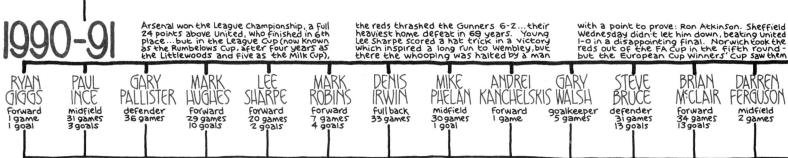

PAUL INCE	GARY PALLISTER	MARK HUGHES	LEE SHARPE	MARK ROBINS	VIV ANDERSON	MIKE PHELAN	LEE MARTIN	GARY WALSH	STEVE BRUCE	BRIAN McCLAIR	MAL DONAGHY
Midfield 25 games	defender 35 games 3 goals	forward 36 games 13 goals	forward 13 games 1 goal	forward 10 games 7 goals	full back 14 games	midfield 38 games 1 goal	defender 28 games	goalkeeper 0 games	defender 34 games 3 goals	forward 37 games 5 goals	defender 13 games

During the summer, Ferguson zapped up his defence with a real bargain- Denis Irwin, purchased from Oldham Athletic for £625,000. He also promoted to the first team a lad who had joined United as a 16 year old apprentice...his son Darren. 1990/91 would be an especially memorable season for Mark Hughes, voted the PFA Footballer of the Year...again (he'd also won the title in 1989), and Lee Sharpe, voted the PFA Young Player of the Year. Nor would Steve Bruce forget banging in 13 goals - plus six more in Cup matches - a record for a defender. Before the season began, England lost the World Cup semi-final on penalties, Gazza cried, and the fat man sang. A bold new decade!

1990-91

Arsenal won the League Championship, a full 24 points above United, who finished in 6th place...but in the League Cup (now known as the Rumbelows Cup, after four years as the Littlewoods and five as the Milk Cup), the reds thrashed the Gunners 6-2...their heaviest home defeat in 69 years. Young Lee Sharpe scored a hat trick in a victory which inspired a long run to Wembley, but there the whooping was halted by a man with a point to prove: Ron Atkinson. Sheffield Wednesday didn't let him down, beating United 1-0 in a disappointing final. Norwich took the reds out of the FA Cup in the fifth round - but the European Cup Winners' Cup saw them

RYAN GIGGS	PAUL INCE	GARY PALLISTER	MARK HUGHES	LEE SHARPE	MARK ROBINS	DENIS IRWIN	MIKE PHELAN	ANDREI KANCHELSKIS	GARY WALSH	STEVE BRUCE	BRIAN McCLAIR	DARREN FERGUSON
Forward 1 game 1 goal	midfield 31 games 3 goals	defender 36 games	forward 29 games 10 goals	Forward 20 games 2 goals	Forward 7 games 4 goals	full back 33 games 1 goal	midfield 30 games	forward 1 game	goalkeeper 5 games	defender 31 games 13 goals	forward 34 games 13 goals	midfield 2 games

1989–90

Back Row (l/r)
Lee Martin, Lee Sharpe, Mike Phelan, Viv Anderson, Steve Bruce, Paul Ince, Neil Webb, Gary Pallister

Middle Row (l/r)
Archie Knox, Alex Ferguson, Mike Duxbury, Jim Leighton, Mal Donaghy, Jim McGregor, Norman Davies

Front Row (l/r)
Brian McClair, Clayton Blackmore, Russell Beardsmore, Bryan Robson, Danny Wallace, Mark Robins, Ralph Milne, Mark Hughes

an assumed impossible away FA Cup third round tie scheduled at Nottingham Forest, Ferguson's name was on the chopper. Behind the scenes, however, it was realised that Fergie was getting it together. The

youth system had been revitalised, discipline restored, and Bobby Charlton in particular argued that it would all come right in time. It came right sooner than anyone expected ...Forest were beaten, thanks to young

Mark Robins, and so began a fantasy march to Wembley. Just as nothing went right in the league (ending in 13th place, dangerously close to relegation - as Liverpool won, again), then nothing went wrong in the Cup. Drawn away

in every round, the reds nonetheless powered past Hereford, Newcastle and Sheffield United to meet and beat Oldham (after a replay) in the semi-final. At Wembley, they met Crystal Palace...managed by Steve Coppell.

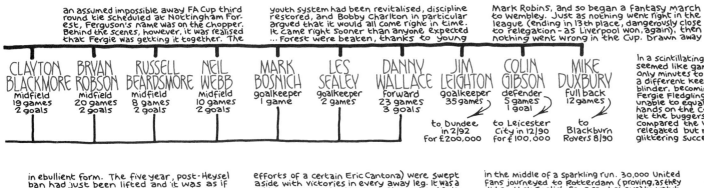

CLAYTON BLACKMORE	BRYAN ROBSON	RUSSELL BEARDSMORE	NEIL WEBB	MARK BOSNICH	LES SEALEY	DANNY WALLACE	JIM LEIGHTON	COLIN GIBSON	MIKE DUXBURY
midfield 19 games 2 goals	midfield 20 games 2 goals	midfield 8 games 2 goals	midfield 10 games 2 goals	goalkeeper 1 game	goalkeeper 2 games	forward 23 games 3 goals	goalkeeper 35 games → to Dundee in 2/92 For £200,000	defender 5 games 1 goal → to Leicester City in 12/90 for £100,000	full back 12 games → to Blackburn Rovers 8/90

In a scintillating final, Ian Wright scored twice for Palace - and it seemed like game-over until Mark Hughes forced a replay with only minutes to go. Five days later, United took the field with a different keeper, Les Sealey, on loan from Luton. He played a blinder, becoming an instant Old Trafford hero. A belter from Fergie Fledgling Lee Martin put United ahead and Palace were unable to equalise. The look on Ferguson's face as he got his hands on the Cup mixed orgasmic delight with intense relief... let the buggers criticise me now! Those with longer memories compared the victory to that in 1963, when United were almost relegated but rallied to win at Wembley, thus sparking 5 years of glittering success. Few dared to believe it could happen again!

in ebullient form. The five year, post-Heysel ban had just been lifted and it was as if they had never been away. Pecsi Munkas, Wrexham and Montpellier (who had won the French Cup the previous year, thanks to the

efforts of a certain Eric Cantona) were swept aside with victories in every away leg. It was a pattern repeated in the semi-final when Legia Warsaw were hammered 3-1 in Poland....but the final promised tougher opposition: Barcelona,

in the middle of a sparkling run. 30,000 United fans journeyed to Rotterdam (proving, as they did so, that English fans can behave) to watch Mark Hughes score two magnificent goals in an improbable, glorious win. United were back!

Late in the season, two future superstars made their debut. On May 11, in the penultimate game, fans got their first tantalising glimpse of the meteoric Andrei Kanchelskis, a Ukranian winger who'd made his reputation with Dynamo Kiev and Shakhytor Donetsk, and whose transfer fee was shrouded in mystery. A week earlier, in a dreamlike first game as a starter, 17 year old Ryan Giggs scored the winning goal against Manchester City, in front of 45,000 punters at Old Trafford. Just a hint of things to come. Born in Cardiff, Giggs played for both Salford and England Schoolboys - and had been on the United books since the age of 14. Unphased by extravagant comparisons with George Best, he kept his cool to capture the PFA Young Player of the Year award in both 1992 and 1993. To even the casual observer, it was quite obvious that United were on the brink of greatness!

CLAYTON BLACKMORE	BRYAN ROBSON	LEE MARTIN	NEIL WEBB	MAL DONAGHY	LES SEALEY	DANNY WALLACE	VIV ANDERSON	RUSSELL BEARDSMORE	MARK BOSNICH	NEIL WHITWORTH
midfield 35 games 4 goals	midfield 15 games 1 goal	defender 7 games → to Aston Villa 7/91	midfield 31 games 3 goals	defender 17 games → to Birmingham City in 10/93 For £400,000	goalkeeper 31 games	forward 13 games 3 goals → to Sheffield Wednesday in 1/91	full back 1 game → to AFC Bournemouth in 6/93	midfield 5 games	goalkeeper 2 games → returned home to Australia in 6/91	defender 1 game → to Kilmarnock in 9/94

1990–91

Back Row (l/r)
Mal Donaghy, Lee Sharpe, Viv Anderson, Les Sealey, Jim Leighton, Mike Phelan, Neil Webb, Steve Bruce

Middle Row (l/r)
Jim McGregor, Archie Knox, Colin Gibson, Brian McClair, Clayton Blackmore, Russell Beardsmore, Paul Ince, Ralph Milne, Norman Davies

Front Row (l/r)
Danny Wallace, Denis Irwin, Mark Robins, Bryan Robson, Alex Ferguson, Mark Hughes, Gary Pallister, Lee Martin

1991-92

In May 1991, the club underwent the most comprehensive financial restructuring in its 89 year history. From now on, it would be known as Manchester United PLC. The share capital raised by the new venture enabled the club to formulate ambitious plans for the redevelopment of the Stretford End as an all-seater stand. The following summer, the terraces would be demolished - much to the dismay of many.

The team which took the field against Notts County, in the first game of the season, had cost over £10 million to put together. Over the next year, United would win the following ... the European Super Cup (beating Champions Cup holders Red Star Belgrade somewhat fortuitously), the FA Youth Cup, both the PFA awards (the senior gong to Gary Pallister and the junior to Ryan Giggs), and - for the first time in the club's history - the League Cup!

But it is a season that will be forever remembered for what wasn't won...the Championship. What rankled was that, unlike in 1988, United weren't distant runners-up. This time the title could,

PETER SCHMEICHEL	RYAN GIGGS	PAUL INCE	GARY PALLISTER	MARK HUGHES	LEE SHARPE	PAUL PARKER	DENIS IRWIN	MIKE PHELAN	ANDREI KANCHELSKIS	GARY WALSH	STEVE BRUCE	BRIAN McCLAIR
goalkeeper 40 games	forward 32 games 4 goals	midfield 31 games 3 goals	defender 37 games 1 goal	forward 38 games 11 goals	forward 8 games 1 goal	defender 24 games	full back 37 games 4 goals	midfield 14 games	forward 28 games 4 goals	goalkeeper 2 games	defender 37 games 5 goals	forward 41 games 18 goals

1992-93

Away from Old Trafford, summer 92 was a busy one. While Turnip Taylor was busily engineering England's humiliation in the European Championships in Sweden, the leading clubs broke away from the Football League and announced the formation of the FA Premier League. Their first action was to sell exclusive live broadcasting rights to Sky TV for an enormous figure. Thus United no longer had any ambition to become champions of Division One (the new name for the old Division Two)...they now set their sights on topping the Premier League. And they did it at their first attempt - by a convincing margin of 10 points! The day it became clear that their nearest rivals Aston Villa had been mathematic-

CLAYTON BLACKMORE	ERIC CANTONA	PETER SCHMEICHEL	RYAN GIGGS	PAUL INCE	GARY PALLISTER	MARK HUGHES	LEE SHARPE	PAUL PARKER	DENIS IRWIN	MIKE PHELAN	ANDREI KANCHELSKIS	GARY WALSH	STEVE BRUCE	BRIAN McCLAIR
midfield 12 games	forward 21 games 9 goals	goalkeeper 42 games	forward 40 games 9 goals	midfield 41 games 6 goals	defender 42 games 1 goal	forward 41 games 15 goals	forward 27 games 1 goal	defender 31 games 1 goal	full back 40 games 5 goals	midfield 5 games	forward 14 games 3 goals	goalkeeper 0 games	defender 42 games 5 goals	forward 41 games 9 goals

to Middlesbrough in 5/94

1991–92

Back Row (l/r)
Brian McClair, Paul Ince, Ryan Giggs, Russell Beardsmore, Darren Ferguson

Middle Row (l/r)
Jim McGregor, Andrei Kanchelskis, Steve Bruce, Mike Phelan, Jim Leighton, Peter Schmeichel, Gary Pallister, Neil Webb, Lee Sharpe, Norman Davies

Front Row (l/r)
Danny Wallace, Clayton Blackmore, Paul Parker, Brian Kidd, Bryan Robson, Alex Ferguson, Lee Martin, Denis Irwin, Mark Hughes

should, ought to have been delivered to the Old Trafford trophy room for the first time in 25 years. Instead (swallow hard, take 3 aspirins and lie down in a darkened room before saying it) the championship trophy was gift-wrapped and delivered on a plate over the Pennines to Leeds. In August, the latest step in his quest to assemble the best team in the world had seen Ferguson sign Paul Parker and Peter Schmeichel. The former was a West Ham lad who'd worked his way into an England youth cap while playing for Fulham and full international regalia after moving on to Queens Park Rangers. At the age of 27, he was worth £1·7 million when he joined United. A recent Danish Footballer Of The Year, the 6'4" Schmeichel joined from Copenhagen-based Brondby for a fee of £500,000. This meant that Gary Walsh, fit again after an ankle injury and subsequent treatment kept him out of the reckoning for a couple of seasons, barely got a look in again this year... but he still hung on in there.

DARREN FERGUSON	CLAYTON BLACKMORE	BRYAN ROBSON	LEE MARTIN	NEIL WEBB	MAL DONAGHY	MARK ROBINS
midfield 2 games	midfield 19 games 3 goals	midfield 26 games 4 goals	defender 0 games	midfield 29 games 3 goals	defender 16 games	forward 1 game
				to Nottingham Forest in 11/92 for £800,000	to Chelsea in 8/92 for £100,000	to Norwich City in 8/92 for £800,000

In the weeks around the new year, United met the recently promoted Leeds (it was only their second season back in Division One) at Elland Road in all three domestic competitions: the League Cup tie was won 3-1, the FA Cup game 1-0, and the league encounter was drawn. At the end of the season, most reds would have happily sacrificed both cup victories for 3 league points. The FA Cup campaign was not to last much longer - in the fourth round, a penalty shoot-out saw them go down to Southampton. (A certain Alan Shearer scored the Saints' winner). The League (ok, Rumbelows) Cup, though, provided sweet recompense for last season. After beating Middlesbrough (a close extra-time affair) in the semi-final - a game at which the breath defying "Ferguson's red and white army" mantra was born on the terraces - Brian Clough's Nottingham Forest were sunk by a Brian McClair goal. But the cup run led to acute fixture congestion, and the reds were faced with playing their last six league games in 16 days. In order to preserve tired limbs, Ferguson tinkered with his line-up, a home game was lost, nerves set in and, despite being ahead at the final bend, the title was blown. In the press, it was widely reckoned that Alex Ferguson would never now win the title, having communicated his agitation to the players in the final furlong. Oh no?

ally ruled out of contention, United weren't playing - but the sense of elation in the red zones of Manchester was so profound that on hearing the news, thousands flocked to Old Trafford, just to be there at such a glorious, triumphal moment. Players arrived too... Lee Sharpe was lifted shoulder high. The last two games of the season, both won, passed by in a blur of red and white. Champions! The previous summer, such jubilation had seemed an unlikely dream. Over the break, the reds failed to land Alan Shearer, the hottest property around ...he chose newly promoted (and heavily financed) Blackburn instead. In his place came the svelte Dion Dublin - Cambridge United's top goalscorer - for a transfer fee of £1 million. After three games of the new campaign, two of them at Old Trafford in front of an empty space that was once famed as the most vibrant terrace in football, United were bottom without a win. A revival was spurred on by a winning Dublin goal at Southampton - but then he broke his leg, and a run of 7 matches without a win suggested a sad winter.

DARREN FERGUSON	DION DUBLIN	BRYAN ROBSON	LEE MARTIN
midfield 15 games	forward 3 games 1 goal	midfield 5 games 1 goal	defender 0 games

A second round dismissal from the League Cup (now called the Coca Cola Cup, god help us) at the hands of Aston Villa, and removal from the UEFA Cup, on penalties away at Torpedo Moscow, added to the gloom and doom...but then, on 26 November 1992, Alex Ferguson achieved a stunning coup, picking up Eric Cantona from Leeds for £1·2 million. The Parisian - a graduate of Auxerre, Bordeaux, Marseille, Montpellier and Nimes - had only been at Leeds for 10 months...but his effect on United cannot be overstated. He scored goals, he executed match winning passes, and more importantly instilled a confidence...as soon as he arrived, everything seemed to slot into place: Kanchelskis and Giggs tore down the wings, Ince blossomed into the best midfielder in the country, and Hughes was playing the most inspired football of his career. More than just a player, Cantona became the United talisman - and, incidentally, the first footballer to exert a rock star's influence on teen fashion: as soon as they saw him on TV, boys everywhere turned up their collars. On a roll, United started winning games with a panache the supporters fancied was their birthright. There were aberrations, like losing away to Sheffield United in the fifth round of the FA Cup (in grim new kit, the third of the season), but mainly it was scintillating stuff. As the climax approached, instead of folding as they had the previous year, United pulled away from Norwich and Villa. Thanks to Sky, who scheduled games at all sorts of odd times in the week, Villa's last chance to catch United was played live on TV on Bank Holiday Monday afternoon. Not daring to sit and watch, Alex Ferguson was on the golf course when he heard the news. Fittingly it was Bryan Robson who scored the last goal of the season. League champions!

1992–93

Ryan Giggs

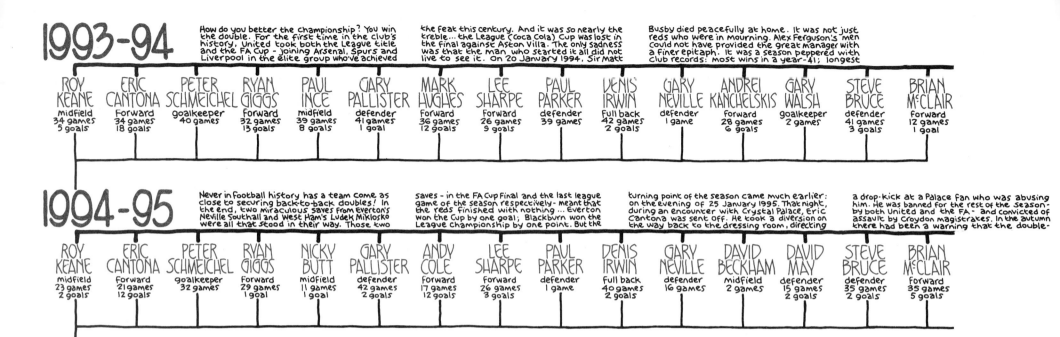

1993-94

How do you better the championship? You win the double. For the first time in the club's history, United took both the League title and the FA Cup – joining Arsenal, Spurs and Liverpool in the elite group who've achieved

the feat this century. And it was so nearly the treble... the League (Coca Cola) Cup was lost in the final against Aston Villa. The only sadness was that the man who started it all did not live to see it. On 20 January 1994, Sir Matt

Busby died peacefully at home. It was not just reds who were in mourning. Alex Ferguson's men could not have provided the great manager with a finer epitaph. It was a season peppered with club records: most wins in a year–41; longest

ROY KEANE	ERIC CANTONA	PETER SCHMEICHEL	RYAN GIGGS	PAUL INCE	GARY PALLISTER	MARK HUGHES	LEE SHARPE	PAUL PARKER	DENIS IRWIN	GARY NEVILLE	ANDREI KANCHELSKIS	GARY WALSH	STEVE BRUCE	BRIAN McCLAIR
midfield 34 games 5 goals	Forward 34 games 18 goals	goalkeeper 40 games	forward 32 games 13 goals	midfield 39 games 8 goals	defender 41 games 1 goal	Forward 36 games 12 goals	Forward 26 games 9 goals	defender 39 games	Full back 42 games 2 goals	defender 1 game	forward 28 games 6 goals	goalkeeper 2 games	defender 41 games 3 goals	Forward 12 games 1 goal

1994-95

Never in football history has a team come as close to securing back-to-back doubles! In the end, two miraculous saves from Everton's Neville Southall and West Ham's Ludek Miklosko were all that stood in their way. Those two

saves – in the FA Cup Final and the last league game of the season respectively – meant that the reds finished with nothing ... Everton won the Cup by one goal; Blackburn won the League championship by one point. But the

turning point of the season came much earlier: on the evening of 25 January 1995. That night, during an encounter with Crystal Palace, Eric Cantona was sent off. He took a diversion on the way back to the dressing room, directing

a drop-kick at a Palace fan who was abusing him. He was banned for the rest of the season- by both United and the FA - and convicted of assault by Croydon magistrates. In the autumn there had been a warning that the double-

ROY KEANE	ERIC CANTONA	PETER SCHMEICHEL	RYAN GIGGS	NICKY BUTT	GARY PALLISTER	ANDY COLE	LEE SHARPE	PAUL PARKER	DENIS IRWIN	GARY NEVILLE	DAVID BECKHAM	DAVID MAY	STEVE BRUCE	BRIAN McCLAIR
midfield 23 games 2 goals	Forward 21 games 12 goals	goalkeeper 32 games	Forward 29 games 1 goal	midfield 11 games 1 goal	defender 42 games 2 goals	Forward 17 games 12 goals	Forward 26 games 3 goals	defender 1 game	Full back 40 games 2 goals	defender 16 games	midfield 2 games	defender 15 games 2 goals	defender 35 games 2 goals	Forward 35 games 5 goals

1993–94

Back Row (l/r)
Andrei Kanchelskis, Mike Phelan, Eric Cantona, Peter Schmeichel, Les Sealey, Gary Pallister, Dion Dublin, Lee Sharpe

Middle Row (l/r)
Norman Davies, Brian McClair, Denis Irwin, Ryan Giggs, Lee Martin, Darren Ferguson, Roy Keane, Mark Hughes, Jim McGregor

Front Row (l/r)
Danny Wallace, Clayton Blackmore, Alex Ferguson, Steve Bruce, Bryan Robson, Brian Kidd, Paul Ince, Paul Parker

unbeaten run - 34 games; longest sequence of away victories - 7; lowest number of league defeats - 4. Like Linford Christie, the team leapt from the blocks, sprinting to an apparently unassailable position at the head of the league by Christmas. Roy Keane had been added to the midfield over summer – a strong competitor signed from Nottingham Forest for a club and English record fee of £3.75 million. His role was to replace the

DARREN FERGUSON	DION DUBLIN	BRYAN ROBSON	LEE MARTIN	MIKE PHELAN	COLIN McKEE
midfield	forward	midfield	defender	midfield	forward
1 game	1 game	10 games	1 game	1 game	1 game
	1 goal	1 goal			
to Wolverhampton Wanderers in 1/94 for £250,000	to Coventry City 9/94 for £1.95 million	to Middlesbrough 5/94	to Celtic in 1/94 for £350,000	to West Bromwich Albion in 6/94	to Kilmarnock in 9/94

departing Bryan Robson, who was off to be player/manager of Middlesbrough after a long and illustrious United career: 12 years, 434 appearances, 97 goals. Two other players, both of whom had joined United as trainees, made their debuts in the last game of the season: Gary Neville and Colin McKee. Ferguson was voted Manager of the Year for the second successive time, and Eric Cantona was the PFA Player of the Year. Indeed, in United's year of triumph, Cantona was the conductor – pulling strings, supplying passes, scoring goals, leading the team through an autumn of untarnished joy. Almost. Back in the competition United have always held in highest regard, the team made a complete hash of the European Cup - losing to Galatasaray of Turkey in the second round. At the end of the turbulent second leg in Istanbul, Cantona was sent off. Worse, the United fans

who travelled with the team were treated disgracefully: herded about, arrested and deported. Six spent a fortnight in jail. But failure was soon forgotten as the reds returned to take the domestic season apart. Few teams could survive under the relentless assault of Kanchelskis, Giggs, Hughes and Cantona – a front line that rolled off the tongue with the same relish as Charlton, Best and Law once had. Comparisons with the old days were frequent.... the 5-0 defeat inflicted on Sheffield Wednesday was reckoned by many observers to have been the finest performance by a United team since 1967, and the 3-0 win over Wimbledon in the cup included a Denis Irwin goal which rounded off a 21-pass move, thought by those

who saw it to have been the slickest in red history. Typically, though, the team frayed their supporters' nerves on the way. There was a horrible mid-season wobble... Schmeichel was sent off in an FA Cup game against Charlton, Cantona was sent off in successive matches, and Blackburn began to breathe down the collars of the players' personalised shirts, bearing their names for the first time. In the end, though, you wondered what the panic was about: the double was achieved with ease...an 8 point gap over Blackburn in the League, and a 4-0 thrashing of Chelsea in the FA Cup Final. The team which won at Wembley that day could justifiably be considered the finest United team of any era...but they would never play together again.

winners would not be quite the same force without their orchestrator. A reserve team of Fergie's Fledglings, minus Cantona, had been brushed aside by Newcastle United in the third round of the Coca Cola Cup. Worse, though, was their experience in the European Cup. Seeded, they were placed directly into the Champions League - but with Cantona suspended after indiscretions in Turkey, the team was hammered 0-4 by Barcelona and then lost 1-3

PAUL SCHOLES	PHILIP NEVILLE	SIMON DAVIES	KEITH GILLESPIE	PAUL INCE	MARK HUGHES	ANDREI KANCHELSKIS	GARY WALSH
forward	defender	midfield	forward	midfield	forward	forward	goalkeeper
6 games	1 game	3 games	3 games	36 games	33 games	25 games	10 games
5 goals			1 goal	5 goals	8 goals	14 goals	
			to Newcastle Utd in 1/95 for £1 million	to Inter Milan in 6/95 for £7 million	to Chelsea in 6/95 for £1.5 million	to Everton in 8/95 for £5 million	to Middlesbrough in 8/95 for £250,000

to Gothenburg. Even with Cantona, the cynics suggested, United might have struggled, their potency undermined by a stupid UEFA rule which restricted the number of foreigners in teams and counted Scots, Welsh and Irishmen as foreigners.

In January, a fortnight before the Cantona incident, Alex Ferguson broke the bank to buy the prolific goalscorer Andy Cole from Newcastle for £6 million, plus the young Northern Ireland winger Keith Gillespie - valued at £1 million. The plan was for Cole to form a championship-winning strike force with Cantona, taking maximum advantage of every chance the Frenchman created...but in the event, they only played together twice. Cole proved his worth by scoring five goals in a record breaking 9-0 win over Ipswich. The season's other big signing was David May who joined from Blackburn Rovers during the summer for £1.4 million.

A 4-0 revenge win over Galatasaray was scant consolation for a campaign which started with such high hopes. The final saw Ajax - three time winners in the early seventies - beat current holders AC Milan.

Three favourites - Ince, Hughes and Kanchelskis - all left Old Trafford at the end of the season, much to the chagrin of fans, and goalkeeper Gary Walsh found a first team place at Middlesbrough after a frustrating decade. However, there was ample satisfaction to be drawn from the emergence of a fine crop of young players from United's fertile nursery: Paul Scholes, David Beckham, Nicky Butt, Simon Davies and a second Neville brother, Philip. Of the £15 million accrued from his summer sales, Alex Ferguson would spend only £400,000 – on Tony Coton, a goalkeeper from Manchester City.

1994–95

Back Row (l/r)
Mark Hughes, Dion Dublin, Lee Sharpe, Eric Cantona, Keith Gillespie, Gary Pallister, Nicky Butt, Brian McClair, Chris Casper

Front Row (l/r)
Andrei Kanchelskis, Peter Schmeichel, David May, Steve Bruce, Brian Kidd, Paul Ince, Ryan Giggs

1995-96

At half-time in their first league match of the season, United's chances of success looked as grey as their grim new away kit....3 - 0 down at Aston Villa. No Hughes, Kanchelskis or Ince - and Cantona sitting in the stand,

two months of his ban remaining. To many observers, there seemed little prospect of glory: "you win nothing with kids" was how Alan Hansen dismissed United's chances on the first Match of The Day. But 48 games

later, Alex Ferguson had achieved history! His lads had won the Premiership and the FA Cup, becoming the first English team to complete a double Double. And what a team they were: home-grown, young

and dynamic. In September 94, Port Vale had complained to the authorities that United had deliberately fielded an under-strength side against them in a Coca Cola Cup tie: 18 months later, seven of that team were euphorically

ROY KEANE	ERIC CANTONA	PETER SCHMEICHEL	RYAN GIGGS	NICKY BUTT	GARY PALLISTER	ANDY COLE	LEE SHARPE	PAUL PARKER	DENIS IRWIN	GARY NEVILLE	DAVID BECKHAM	DAVID MAY	TERRY COOKE	BRIAN McCLAIR	PAUL SCHOLES	PHILIP NEVILLE
midfield	forward	goalkeeper	forward	midfield	defender	forward	forward	defender	full back	defender	midfield	defender	forward	forward	forward	defender
29 games	31 games	36 games	30 games	31 games	21 games	32 games	20 games	5 games	31 games	30 games	26 games	11 games	1 game	12 games	16 games	21 games
6 goals	14 goals		11 goals	2 goals	1 goal	11 goals	4 goals		1 goal		7 goals	1 goal		3 goals	10 goals	

1995–96

Back Row (l/r)
Andy Cole, Brian McClair, Roy Keane, Gary Neville, David Beckham, Gary Pallister, Nicky Butt, Ryan Giggs, Eric Cantona, Brian Kidd

Front Row (l/r)
Phil Neville, Denis Irwin, Peter Schmeichel, Steve Bruce, David May, Paul Scholes

running round Wembley with the Cup! It took a while to get into stride: Cole couldn't score; the defence suffered injury problems; there were early exits in the Coca Cola Cup (after an embarrassing 3-0 home defeat to York) and the UEFA Cup (to the

SIMON DAVIES	KEVIN PILKINGTON	STEVE BRUCE	WILLIAM PRUNIER
forward 1 game	goalkeeper 2 games	defender 30 games 1 goal	defender 2 games
	→ to Birmingham City in 5/96 free transfer		→ on loan from Marseille, to whom he returned

unknown Russians Rotor Volgograd); and in the league, Newcastle, who spent over £20 million on players in the year, were simply flying. The strategy within the club seemed to be: everything will be all right when King Eric gets back .... and it was! On October 1st, Eric ended his 9 month suspension and scored (but of course) against Liverpool in his first game. It was immediately clear that he was fit, hungry and determined; but more than that self-disciplined, apparently well aware that this was his last chance not to compromise his talent. Even with the Frenchman, however, United had a bad Yuletide - losing at Leeds, Liverpool and Spurs. Significantly, though, they beat runaway leaders Newcastle with a performance of real power. Then, after

surviving with a late equaliser (from Cantona, who else) in the FA Cup 3rd round against Sunderland, they put together an astonishing new year run. With Schmeichel dominant (he headed a goal in Europe!), Philip Neville emerging as the best full back in Britain and May filling in resolutely for Bruce, the back line was solid; in midfield no-one could beat Keane and Butt; out on the wings Beckham was smooth and capable, and Giggs was back to his elegant, tantalising best. Up front, Scholes was popping them in - and controlling the whole operation was Cantona, unstoppable, converting goal after goal. It took time, but Newcastle were gradually pulled back, their 12 point lead slowly wilting. The turning

point was the Newcastle/Man Utd league match at St James Park, where the home side were undefeated...until Cantona and the lads paid a visit. The Geordies began to collapse, losing games as their fans blubbed openly at the missed chances - while United powered on remorselessly. The Premiership was settled only in the last game - away at Bryan Robson's Middlesbrough. "We won the league again, Down by the Riverside", chanted fans. In the FA Cup, meanwhile, United galloped past Reading, Manchester City, Southampton and Chelsea to reach a third successive final - against the familiar enemy Liverpool. The Cup was popped into the trophy cabinet with a splendid goal by King Eric, the Footballer Of The Year. Alan Hansen prepared to eat his words!

The 1996 FA Cup Final

Eric Cantona raises the FA Cup in triumph

Manchester United 1 – 0 Liverpool

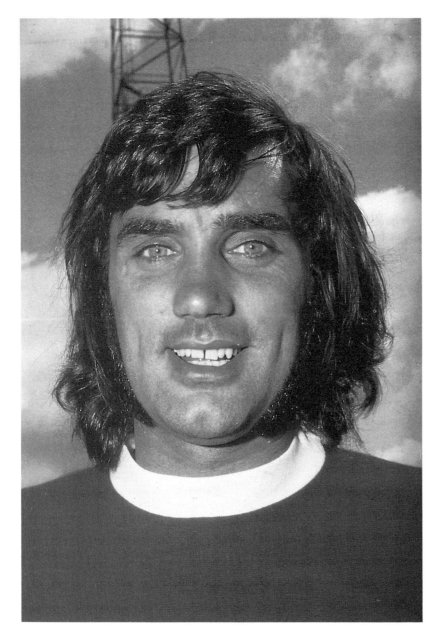

George Best

Alex Stepney

Ryan Giggs and Paul Ince celebrate a goal for Manchester United

Bryan Robson receives an award from Denis Law

Bobby Charlton

Gordon Strachan

Picture Credits

The Publisher would like to thank the following for providing photographs and for permission to reproduce copyright material. While every effort has been made to trace and acknowledge copyright holders, we would like to apologise should there be any errors or omissions.

News Team, Zone Ltd, Action Images, Allsport, Colorsport, Empics Ltd, Associated Press

MANCHESTER UNITED FAMILY TREE

(SLEEVE NOTE ON HOW TO BUY POSTERS)

Pete Frame's "Manchester United Family Tree" (1955–95) is also available in the form of two giant, 2ft x 3 ft posters.

If you have enjoyed this book, then you'll find the posters – each of which cover twenty years of Manchester United's history – a stunning addition to your wall.

With devil-red print, surrounded by photographs of stars past and present, the posters clearly and attractively chart the eras 1955–75 and 1975–1995.

They can **only** be purchased from:

B.D.P.
3–4 Little Portland Street
London W1N 6BD

Telephone 0171 323 3003 (Visa and Mastercard credit card orders)

Price £10 (+ £1.50 p&p) each